EMPOWERING ABILITIES

- Voices of the Voiceless –

- Abilities –

"Possession of the qualities required to do something"

Chapters

Acknowledgements

Hello to you the reader and thank you first and foremost for making the conscious decision to read this book. We hope you enjoy it!

I feel that it is of utmost importance for each of us to acknowledge every individual who has crossed our paths within this journey we call life, whether it was a positive interaction or an unbeneficial one. During and after each of these daily interaction you can choose to grow from each experience, and choose to be grateful, right?

Generally speaking the acknowledgements section within most books is a place where an author gets to thank those who have contributed in some way to the production of the book in question…and also in some cases the authors speak directly to the audience…thanking them for taking the time to read their book.

An author knows that books are created to be read, and that that is their ultimate purpose.

So once again, thank you for choosing this book to read, whether you are holding a physical 'paperback' copy or have opted to read it as an eBook. Regardless, I am glad that you are here, and I trust that you are interested in the material within the following chapters…interested enough to continue turning the pages to seek more of an insight into the lives…and challenges of these incredible authors. Speaking of which… this book would not have been made possible without the incredible people involved in its production…and subsequent success.

I am very grateful to ALL of the authors involved…they showed up as 'authorly' and their authenticity shone through. They ALL had the willingness to not give up. They willingly opened up and gave an insight into an aspect of their lives that is of great importance to them…hopefully this will shine through within the following chapters. They shared their stories and have been gifted this wonderful opportunity to grow in confidence, feel proud in all they have achieved, and ***build up more virtual social connections during a time when the world was being told to limit its physical social interactions.***

For me I am particularly proud as most of the authors never engaged in such a large scale project before…let alone write a chapter in a collaboration book! Some of them came at me and Patrick with a sense of disbelief regarding their true capabilities. However, both Patrick and I saw their potential. I saw the fact that they ALL had an Empowering story to share… and I saw it even more so when they said that they have 'nothing to write about' or that they 'are not able to write' etc. However, I saw how they thrived at facing their individual obstacles, and I felt so blessed for their trust, patience, enthusiasm, and respect in both Patrick and I.

I wish to thank the following authors:
Cheryl Hilson, Christian Formosa, Lorraine Maher, Alan Fay, Michelle Rooney, Paul Gantley, Emer Concannon, Kathryn Hogan, Aine Lawlor, Niamh Dunphy and Jennifer Mccann.

To see the pride and smile of joy in all of their faces as we slowly began piecing together their chapters was so exciting. I am delighted that I also expanded my reach for this book to include authors from outside Ireland…and even outside of the continent of Europe.

I want to thank my incredible husband Patrick Hogan, We have worked so well as a team these past number of years…long may in continue. I am very thankful for Patrick. When Patrick sees the potential in something, he does not give up. He constantly shows up as dedicated, wise, and definitely strong.

During the early stage of this book being put together Patrick was working from home while also studying for his Honours Degree…also from home. In 2021 he successfully completed his Degree while continuing to work from home. Patrick has given his time, energy, and enthusiasm to Empowering Abilities….and to this book.

Patrick is so committed, loyal, and has such a big heart. He showed patience, kindness and listening skills. He took on a tough role which he took on knowing that by doing so was an opportunity for him to grow within himself and develop his interaction and strategic skills.

I am so Amazed by Patrick.

I would like to take this opportunity to thank a colleague of Patricks, Emma Levey-Neilson, who kindly proofread the majority of this book and recommended changes where applicable.

Also, Dylan Hogan who assisted Patrick with the final phases of the book cover.

Lastly, I want to thank Sandra Dillion for her wonderful support and for organising a pre-launch in November 2021.

 I met Sandra spontaneously after hearing her on a radio station and I knew from listening to her that I just had to meet this 'wonder woman'. Through meeting Sandra it has opened up my world and I have met a lot more like-minded people.

Sandra has such fabulous qualities about her, and she ALWAYS serves people in the best way possible.

This book all began from an idea…an idea that was inspired by a thought I had while out walking with Patrick one day during the early stages of the Pandemic… just a thought…just a walk.

Kind regards

Tracey Mccann

Empowering Abilities

Testimonial

I would like to congratulate Tracey McCann on another wonderful achievement of publishing her latest book "Empowering Abilities".

Tracey has overcome, with inspiring and powerful dedication her own disability and has now given a voice to many others whose stories are now told in this wonderful book.

These too are amazing stories showing each of the authors own resilience and inner strength that allow them to overcome their individual disabilities and live fulfilling lives that are a remarkable outcome of their determination and endurance.

Tracey's work with others in helping them explore their potential and developing confidence in their abilities is truly outstanding.

Along with Patrick Hogan they have managed to publish a lovely book of stories that deserves to be widely read by anyone with a heart that's beating!

I hope that Empowering Abilities is a great success in itself to go along with so many brilliant other achievements in her life to date.

She continues to amaze us all with her own story and I wish her every success with her continuous work of inspiring others to overcome their disabilities.

Well done Tracey, it's a marvellous piece of work!

Brian Kerr: Patron of Dystonia Ireland and Former Manager of the Republic of Ireland Senior Football Team

Preface

'Empowering'

Firstly, to you the reader, thank you for choosing this book to read.

It is my hope that from reading, and getting to know each of the incredible authors who wrote in this book, you will receive a sense of Empowerment and Motivation within yourself.

It is also my hope that through learning from each individual, and seeing their hidden capabilities, this will unlock the same within you; that you possibly would not have even realised.

Let us now open your eyes to the fact that each unique person with a disability… counts, as do you. While these individuals may have other ways of doing things, and you may not even be aware that a person with whom you interact with on a daily basis has a disability….those disabilities should not…and do not…define us.

Within this book there are a various range of disabilities, however, as the 'parent' of this project, I am not looking at the disabilities. This is because, as this book will demonstrate to you, it is the ability within each author that we must focus on, right?

I am very grateful and privileged to have these authors part of my first 'Empowering Abilities' book…these individuals are the "Voices of the Voiceless".

I wanted to shine a light on these authors as they represent everything that they talk about within their chapters.

Before we begin allow me to introduce myself. My name is Tracey Mccann and I am the CEO of Empowering Abilities. This business involves many different aspects such as my 1-1 6 week Empowering Abilities Coaching Programme, my Empowering Abilities group Programmes, and also my Empowering and Motivating Corporate talks. My aim within all that I do is to help individuals to feel connected with themselves and others, to gain confidence… and ultimately to live the life that they truly deserve. I help individuals discover and develop their hidden potential. I allow each individual discover their ability to do their own inner work, while I am just their guide…guiding them towards leaning into a space of self-recognition, self-pride, and most importantly…self-empowerment.

I am very passionate about what I am doing, and I feel proud of myself because I am succeeding at what I do. When my clients smile and are thankful for my work, and say that it gave them clarity, and the inspiration to keep moving forward with a much clearer view of the positive outcome that they desire, I am filled with gratitude to receive these words of kindness…it is great to know that I have helped…I am achieving my purpose.

The following book first came about before I registered my business…
before I even knew that after planning this book, that literally after a
few months my business would begin to come into formation.
So, let me begin how this book came about.

During the 2020 lockdown, things were just a little bit crazy, would you
say. By March 2020 the situation was so scary and nobody truly
understood exactly what this virus was, or how harmful it could
be….to both the human body…and the global societal structure as a
whole.

When the first lockdown started to kick in, which happened quite
quickly, everything started to close down and restrictions began taking
place. I married my now husband Patrick during the lockdown, in
October 2020. This was after we rearranged our wedding from May to
October in the hope that things would have settled down by October.
Our new plan was not as special to us as our original May wedding (we
had original planned to get married in the venue where we first met
16+ years ago), but we managed to get the day done and then two days
away the following week on a 'mini moon' in a nearby location by the
sea. We could not have our planned and paid for honeymoon to
Ecuador as travel restrictions were in place. Then just as our little mini
moon had ended the hard lockdown came back… pretty much
everything other than food shopping came to a halt.

On the last day of our mini moon we went on a morning stroll to the sea, both feeling all loved up and wanting to hold on to the moment.

Patrick began talking about everything that needed to done and he was talking about this book, I was like "So the mini moon is now over… it's time to put on our working hats again" laughing to myself… and also feeling thankful to have Patrick as enthusiastic as me…he could see the potential and the value that lay within this book.

So, let us go back a bit again, to March 2020. Patrick was now working from home which meant he was around the home more and it was easier for him to assist me as he did not need to travel to and from work every day…we could either choose to use this time, and this opportunity to be wasted… or to be productive. We chose to do what we could, and what felt was right at the time, just like everyone else in the world, including you.

We both became aware of our surroundings and discovered new places to walk too, places that were literally on our door step. I think everyone in the country was like that…discovering new places that we did not even know existed…places within a five kilometre distance of our home. It is only when you are giving the opportunity to look that you discover these 'hidden gems'… and you laugh to yourself thinking "Wow! This was here all along… right under my nose!" Did you experience this too??

While out on our walks I felt more creative than ever, I felt during the stillness and silence that I could hear my thoughts more clearly. I found being out in nature was the perfect opportunity to witness these inspiring thoughts. I felt such a clear vision and ambition towards seeing these visions take shape. I felt that Patrick was tuned in too, and was more creative than ever. We were able to bounce ideas off each other and feel excited about our plans.

Firstly, I came up with my name, Empowering Abilities, which I felt was very fitting.

Patrick came up with "The Voice of the Voiceless" which he explained as meaning an individual who advocates on behalf of those whose 'voices' have been dimmed within society.

This was also very fitting for me, especially as I have speech difficulties, and my verbal communication is that bit more unique.

I felt engulfed in my silence for so long… and yet here I am… stepping out with an empowered mind-set, and the right attitude to succeed in life.

You, the reader, have a voice too. Regardless as to whether individuals can understand you clearly or not…this is beside the point… get people to understand, and let your voice be heard! Free yourself from being in the dark, speak up, and value your trust within. Your voice is empowering, your words are here to embrace, to appreciate and honour.

So, on our walk I heard, in my thoughts, that a book was needed to be written. Not just any book though, but a calibration book…written by Patrick, other people with disabilities, and myself. Using the title "Voices of the Voiceless" to encompass this collection of authors would be very strong and capturing.

It took me a few days to voice this thought to Patrick, as I felt I had to sit with it for a bit myself, and really listen to what it was that I was conceiving.
I felt very happy to express this to Patrick and to receive his natural response of enthusiasm and excitement.

I felt happy with this idea, and the reaction from Patrick, and I began my journey in finding my potential authors. I opened up myself to allow the right people to flow to me...

Patrick and I have spent the past few years learning how to inspire, motivate and empower those who we came into contact with....and we felt that it was time to teach this skill onto others...

Introduction

By Cheryl Hilson

"Empowerment…To have your own choices" – Cheryl Hilson

I am an Australian Disabled woman of 53 years. During these years there have been many changes I have seen. When I was young people with disabilities were educated in a segregated manner. Separate to that of their able-bodied peers. Today however, children with disabilities can be educated within their local schools. They also have access to the same level of opportunities as their able-bodied peers i.e. work, leisure, and as stated previously, education. There are a plentiful amount of opportunities available to the disabled community now-a-day as opposed to what was available when I was young.

When I was young I was hidden from a lot of the negative experiences that every individual will (and should) encounter within their lives. This intentional obstruction of the negative aspects of life and society was simply phrased (by those who were doing so as a form of protection) as "Don't tell Cheryl… she can't cope with it".

Although there have been many changes these days regarding how the disabled community 'fit into' society as a whole there is still a lot more that needs to be done to remove the barriers that still exist in the minds and attitudes of the able-bodied community. There are limitations put in our way… where there not should. In my opinion, the disabled community require more individuals to stand up for our rights…our rights to (at the least) attempt at surpassing those limitations. I feel that we require the use of our collective powerful voices to bring about the much desired change that we seek.

Within the chapters of this book you will find people from both inside and outside the disabled community describing to you their views, their unique perspectives, their struggles, their personal victories…and their lives. Upon reading this book you may tell that to some within the disabled community a disability is not a misfortune…It is simply a challenge that we must overcome. Sometimes we will fail and other times we will succeed…but we will always attempt…at the least. For me, I wish I could know the difference. I taught my daughter and I now teach my grandchildren this simple truth, we all have something about us that makes us unique…We all are faced with situations that test our resources… but it is how we overcome our challenges and learn from them that makes us stronger and resilient enough to move on and become our own unique definition of 'successful' individuals. This applies to whatever it is that we choose to do. Take me and my current situation as an example, I am in TAFE (Technical and Further Education) currently studying community services. I am studying this with the objective of becoming a Disability Advocate… but this does not stop me being able to advocate for others, disabled or otherwise, and assisting wherever my skills and qualifications may be required.

Life is meant to be enjoyed… until the last minute of any adventure or experience that you are having. You are never too old to follow your own dreams. In order to 'set the tone' for the following chapters held within this book allow me to offer my own personal advice…taken from my own personal experience… Do not let anyone or anything stop you from getting the best out of life. You are unique… and you are worth it. As a unique human being it is (in my opinion) essential for you (as a friend once said to me) to show up for yourself.

Lastly, upon reading this book you will be inspired, you will cry, you will love, you will find inner gratitude…and much much more. I am grateful to my friend Tracey and here amazing husband Patrick who have bestowed upon me the great privilege of opening this book up to you, the reader. It has been my honour to do this for them…and for you.

Please enjoy the following voices, speaking loudly and clearly via the written word, showing up for both themselves…and for you.

Yours sincerely

Cheryl Hilson

EMPOWERING ABILITIES

- Voices of the Voiceless –

Chapter 1

- Attitude -

By Tracey Mccann

Introduction

My name is Tracey Mccann, I am a 33 year old disabled woman from Dublin, Ireland, and I am the CEO of Empowering Abilities. This business, although a long time coming, was initially and officially set up in 2020 with the sole purpose of empowering ALL of my clients. One way in which I achieve this is by teaching my clientele how to adopt an 'Attitude of Gratitude'…because attitude is important, as are all of the other traits highlighted in this book. But what is an attitude of gratitude and how did it assist me to achieve all that I have achieved? Allow me to explain.

As indicated above my name is Tracey Mccann and I am living a successful, happy, empowered, free life, because I made a choice to continue on, I chose to continue being my best, I chose to help myself and other people who came across my path. I made this choice despite my challenges that I incurred from a young age…I chose to adopt an attitude of gratitude in all aspects of my life…despite some aspects of my life attempting at pulling me down…disempowering me…destroying my positive, motivated and determined spirit…and ending me in my current form.

Struggling with Attitude

When I was a little girl and even prior to my life being greatly altered by my rare disability known as Dystonia, I really struggled with my identity. I felt as though I did not fit in, that the body I inhabited was not 'correct'. A large amount of challenges occurred for me at such a young age, and these filled me with uncertainty about who I was as an individual. I began distancing myself from others, and blaming myself and other people for my inability to know who I was. When I was younger, I was always full of questions, about myself, and the world around me. I was a deep thinker. Also, I would spend the majority of my earlier years alone, and would spend this time of isolation devoted to negative self-talk. This inner destruction of myself had an outwardly effect too, and manifested itself via repulsive childish behavior, such as bitterness, anger, frustration, and emotional detachment. To outsiders looking in I came across as being emotionally unbalanced, desperate at times, needy, self-loathing, and extremely self-centered.

However, given my young and tender age at the time I also came across very innocent, and was always smiling. I was very shy to let go, even around my own family. People would ask me a question and I would get very embarrassed. My cheeks would go bright red and I would feel my heart begin to race. I desperately wanted the spot light off me. The funny thing is that I could have just been asked a simple innocent question like "how are you?"

During those moments my mind would simply shut off, because if I had replied in the usual standard manner "I'm fine" or "I'm good" Deep down I knew that I would be lying to myself. The truth was that I could not put into the words how I was truly feeling, or even if I did, would the right help be there? This was Ireland in the mid 90's, so there were not as many counselling services available for children as there are now in these modern times. Even with that in mind however, I had been going to a form of counselling, but I struggled with releasing all of my 'demons', and really looking after myself. To be honest, even with this service I still did not know how to help myself. My attitude about myself absolutely stank, it was zero to none. The only time I felt truly free was on my own, wrapped up in my imagination, playing endlessly in my own little innocent and untampered world, or out on family days in the forest. I felt 'ok' playing innocent games with my brothers and cousins. We would run around screaming, I felt truly free and I embraced it, I felt so connected and happy in nature, I felt deeply grounded by being surrounded by the smells and sounds of nature. This always gave me such a happy boost. Being outside in the heart of Mother Nature was my escape, and I always had a desire to want more from this form of escapism. I always felt more of a good feeling about myself during those outings. I felt as though I was becoming stronger, and was beginning to have a love for myself. I embraced the feeling the freedom and began accepting this fact of life, being on earth had and will always have 'ups' and 'downs', Those times spent in nature were equipping me with a valuable lesson which was as follows: Life is a journey of discovery, and within our time on this earth it is up to us all to discover what it is that makes us externally and internally happy, and then develop a positive attitude that guarantees we obtain that happiness

Adopting the RIGHT Attitude

Throughout my early life I faced many extreme physical, emotional, and mental challenges. I have had many moments of feeling more and more isolated and fearful. Yet at times I also felt strong, brave and as though I had to disconnect myself from those negative and unwanted feelings. I would deliberately and consciously instruct myself to believe and have an unproven knowledge that everything would be ok for me. I would tell myself that "I am strong, I've got this" At times however, if I was feeling low and dark negative thoughts would begin to creep in and seemingly cloud over me I was not, I will admit, in the right state to hear anything positive, not even from myself. I always had to be ready and willing. I will say this you, the reader, during moments of feeling very low and or depressed we do not really hear what we feel we should hear. What I mean by that is that we have to **want** to hear positive things about us, and we have to want to know that there is light at the end of our seemingly dark tunnels. However, if we are not in the right state to move forward, then sadly there is no point. We must be ready to accept the fact that we need to change our mindset, change our perspective, and change our attitude. Only then can we begin to work through the process of making lasting change within our external and internal worlds. We control the direction our life's can take, and we control our minds, it is not the other way round. To begin changing our attitudes it is very important that we learn to control our emotions, we must acknowledge our feelings that we encounter on a daily basis, and then move on; this can be done in our own time.

For me personally, what I have learnt is to ask myself good "Why?" questions. My brain would always look for all the reasons why I feel such and such a way, and it is the same for you too. When you are thinking negatively and you ask questions of yourself, you will always receive a negative response. Why? Because your brain loves to be proven right, so subsequently you tell yourself that you have every justifiable reason to feel this way. In my opinion and from my own experience this is why people struggle with moving forward…they constantly seek confirmation from within as to why they are struggling. Many years ago I felt deflated, and worn down from being my own critic. There are many people out there who feel good knocking others and putting them down…why do we allow the outside world to affect our inside world? Besides, in the majority of cases those individuals who do put others down are just masking their own insecurities, and feelings of inadequacy. How does putting others down grow and develop individuals in the right direction? If you are a person who does this then how does it make you feel? It potentially alienates you from people when place a label on them. Do you want to be known as the nasty and judgmental person that you may be perceived as? Do you want people to stay away from you? Well it is the same for how you talk to yourself…what it is that you tell yourself about yourself…right? If we knock ourselves down daily and expect others to listen to us criticizing ourselves we will never repair that supposed 'flaw' within ourselves that we are criticizing. In order to repair our flaws or at the very least begin to identify those flaws we must first approach this exercise from an attitude of purely positive intention i.e. I know what my flaws are, I acknowledge them…but I choose to focus on repairing these flaws from a positive and determined mind-set. This practice comes from one of 'choice'…everything is a choice, happiness is a choice, happiness is not something that we chase in the external world, it exists solely within. For me, I made the choice to change my attitude, embrace life and find ways that make me feel good daily. This was my choice…what is yours?

The Contagiousness of Attitude

What is attitude? To me attitude is a contiguous thing that can greatly affect our perceptions of the world around us, and us as individuals too. This can be a positive effect, or a negative one. Let us focus on the one we all desire, the one we all seek, let us focus on obtaining, and then maintaining a positive attitude. This is an attitude that has the potential to both enhance our lives, and our capabilities to new incredible levels. One of the first steps to achieve this is for you to ALWAYS have an attitude of gratitude i.e. to focus on what you already have.

You must realise that you are the master of our own mind, and also, that you are more than your mind. You are a magnificent human being who can do and be anything you choose. Whatever your ability, you can do everything in your own unique way. This book will highlight each individual author who have contributed within, their own unique brave, intelligent, loving, imaginative, tenacious, self-identifying, equal, and strong way of facing their challenges and subsequently improving their lives. You too have the power within to make the choice, and to know which choice is right and or wrong for you.

Ask yourself…what kind of person do you want to be known as? How do you want to make others feel by being in your presence?

If you feel sad and not good enough, then show kindness to others and do it often, this kindness will reflect back to you 10 fold. In my opinion life is about bringing people 'up' to a state of inner happiness, and not putting them 'down' into a state of self-despair. Smile more and look into people's eyes with compassion and love.

Change your attitude, change your perception and you can change your life. Every day is not going to be perfect for you, you may have knocks or setbacks, you may blame others, and you may feel nothing is working, you may have doubts, and you may even feel like giving up. But what result would that leave you with? Ultimately you may feel alone, you may look at everything wrong with yourself, you may feel disempowered, you may feel exhausted, and all of this may lead you to unintentionally snapping at others.

Once again, change your attitude, change your perception of your life, change how you interact with the individuals you surround yourself with on a daily basis…and change how you interact with yourself. Doing this WILL change your life…trust me…I know…I have done this and have witnessed others doing it too…it works.

Conclusion

Remember, attitude is contagious i.e. having a positive attitude not only affects others around you but also greatly impacts your physical, emotional and mental state. With that in mind, always be the first person who makes YOU laugh out loud today, because laughing is great for the mind and the body. On the other side of that is anger and anger takes away from your whole day. Energy wise, you could feel floored by this negative emotion. If you ever get like this then here is a piece of advice for you….pick yourself up, dust yourself off, laugh like it is no one's business…and always put on a happy face.

Give yourself a real boost of endorphins, which are free to use anytime you choose. Be the best you can be in that perfect soul you were giving. Live each moment embracing the wonderful gifts that you possess within. We are all miracles and we have all got this. You too, have got this.

Chapter 2

- Bravery -

By Christian Formosa

"Showing persistence in the face of adversity is in my opinion true bravery.
It is when you stare at your issues straight in the eyes, be it physical adversities,
or be it mental ones, and you bravely continue along your path… keeping your head
held high throughout"
– Christian Formosa

Introduction

My name is Christian Formosa and I was born on the Island of Gozo in Malta on the 3rd of October 1993. It became immediately apparent from my birth that I had been born with Cerebral Palsy. Prior to my attending school it would be fair to say that I had a happy childhood. I began attending mainstream school at the age of 4-5, and it was not until I reached the age of 8 and was still in my primary school years that my bravery was tested.

It all began with my fellow students calling me names due to my disability. Then, from the age of 10-16 while attending secondary school, this form of bullying continued. A number of my peers from primary school began attending the same secondary school as me. Even though I was victim of this daily verbal abuse from my fellow students I had my own way of dealing with this which basically consisted of me mentally switching between my school life and family life. In other words I did not flag this bullying with neither my family or my teachers in school, the only people who knew about this was myself and the bullies. Over the following years this slowly became my normality. It was not until the age of 17-18 that I began noticing that the abuse was negatively affecting my mental state. I sought out some professional mental health assistance and began my journey dealing with my mental health problems.

When I began my mental health treatment both my parents still did not know for certain what had caused this, they just presumed that I became mentally sick without knowing the reasons why and the full story behind my situation. Neither I, nor my parents realised at the time that due to the daily bullying I endured at such a young age and right into my late teens that I had unwittingly obtained a mental health disorder known as Bipolar.

Mental Health Treatment

Although I began my mental health treatment at the age of 17-18 the frequency of this treatment met neither my needs nor my desire for professional psychological assistance. From 2011 until 2018 I could only go to my doctor for psychological assistance once every 6 months and was only ever issued with medication. In 2012 shortly after starting this treatment I had submitted an application for community mental health assistance which was disqualified due to my living on an island in Malta where this service did not exist. This service was in fact only offered on one island within Malta. I then submitted another application in 2016 which was disqualified also due to the same issue, this motivated me towards fighting for this service, among other services to be available on my Island, the Island of Gozo.

I alone fought hard and bravely for three straight years for the rights of the citizens of Gozo in accessing these much required services. This 'fight' involved me sending numerous emails, certificates and letters of petition to members of the Maltese government, the President of Malta, and anyone who could bring about this change that I so eagerly desired.

Eventually, and thankfully, in 2019 the President of Malta at that time whose name is Marie-Louise Coleiro Preca granted my request; finally I was victorious in the first stage of my one man mission.

The Island of Gozo, with a population of just under 33,000 inhabitants, finally had one of these essential and necessary services made available to them, with this service being a "Community Support Service".

As indicated above the service currently available on the Island of Gozo is just one single service. I am continuing in my battle to obtain the other essential and necessary services to the Island of Gozo.

My Daily Routine

Currently I live in my family home, and am receiving care and therapy for both my mental health disorder alongside physiotherapy for my physical disability, and these keep both my body and mind as healthy as possible. What keeps me motivated however is the continuing battle, which sometimes seems impossible, and can be dispiriting, but ultimately WILL be beneficial to Gozo when I am successful, and I will be successful. I believe in what I am fighting for, and I also believe that as I have succeeded once before in my seemingly uphill and at times difficult challenge made even harder and more frustrating when I have my own mental health issues, I know and **believe** that I WILL **overcome.**

One may question my motives for pursuing these services, and one may come to the conclusion that my reasoning is born out of my needs and requirements, and this conclusive answer that one may arrive at is true to an extent. However, I did not, and am not, continuing to do so purely to satisfy my own wants and needs, but due to me primarily feeling obligated to bravely fight this fight, for **ALL** the citizens of Gozo. Gozo is the place where I was born and despite my difficult schooling years, along with the fact that I am essentially alone in this and without many people with whom I could call friends, it is still the place that I love.

Being Brave in this Lonely World

As I have stated above I would not have had many friends throughout my life, and this makes me firstly feel different to others. Combined with this fact that I have lived with my entire life I also am socially isolated as people within my community do not talk to me. I genuinely believe that this is because they cannot relate to me as a person, they cannot relate to me as a disabled member of society, and they cannot relate to me as a citizen of Malta who is trying to deal with my mental health issues. The reasoning for this is because in Malta, as with many other countries globally, there is a stigma attached to mentally and or physically disabled people as to the capabilities of those individuals.

One day in the early part of 2020 while on YouTube I was seeking some much needed inspiration and motivation to continue in fighting my battles. I came across a video of a disabled woman who was using her disability to her advantage by providing people with her story of courage and bravery in the face of adversity and struggle, and her motivating message. I could immediately relate to everything that this woman spoke about and that video served my need for inspiration and motivation. I decided to take a leap of faith and bravely sought out this woman on social media and proceeded then to send her a friend request. To my delight and surprise she accepted and we have been in communication ever since. This woman's name is Tracey Mccann and it is because of her that I am not only writing this chapter within this amazing book, but also can now say that I have a friend, not just any friend, a friend who I can relate to, and she to me also.

In my honest opinion I believe that this situation that has played out over the past few months is nothing short of a miracle. This newly formed friendship and the sharing of experiences makes me so happy that I clicked the mouse on the 'send friend request' button on that social media platform. I finally feel accepted by another, and also have value from another individual and value from myself.

Conclusion

In my opinion bravery is firstly about not being afraid to be yourself, and secondly it is about having a dream, and pursuing that dream.

It might take weeks, it might take months, or it may even take years to eventually obtain what you are in pursuit of, but as long as you persist on your path, ignoring all the negativity that you will get from others, and or may get from yourself too, you will get there, you will achieve whatever it is that you original set out to achieve years ago. This in my opinion makes all the challenging times that you will face while in pursuit, ultimately worth it in the end. You WILL feel pride, and you WILL feel hungry for more.

Even if you have a physical and or mental disability believe me you can still achieve all that you want to achieve. You may need extra support and assistance yes, but you can still obtain what it is that your heart and mind wishes to obtain.

EMPOWERING ABILITIES

- Voices of the Voiceless –

Chapter 3

- Intelligence -

By Lorraine Maher

"Life is for living

This is how it works:

You're young until you're not.

You love until you don't.

You try until you can't.

You laugh until you cry.

You cry until you laugh

And everyone must breathe

Until their dying breath"- Regina Spektor

Introduction

Hello. My name is Lorraine Maher. I am delighted, honored and proud to have been asked to add my chapter to this amazing book. I hope you enjoy reading my chapter and it gives you some hope for a positive future for you or a loved one.

A Bit of Me and the Family.

I'm thirty five years old and I live in Dublin with my parents. Hopefully I'll be living in my own place soon. I am the second child of four children. I have one older brother and a twin brother and sister, a year younger than me. Disability has been a long time in my family. Both my brothers were born deaf and I was born with a mild form of Cerebral Palsy. To say it was a busy house is an understatement. Three children growing up in the same house with disabilities was no picnic for mum and dad. For myself, having Cerebral Palsy means I am a wheelchair user and I have been all my life, also, the right side of my body does not work as well as the left side; but believe me, I have never let that stop me from living my life to the fullest.

From way back to when I was young, I remember both mum and dad always saying to all of us, "yes you may need to do some things in your everyday life a bit different to everyone else", but when it came to going after anything we wanted in our lives, both mum and dad supported us in every way they could. Mum was a stay at home mother while my Dad was a soldier all his life and that meant he would often be away from home and family life, working in different countries for six months at a time, leaving mum to look after all of us and everything else at home.

Looking back on it all now, I am amazed at how she managed to fit everything in, between hospital appointments with me and/or my brothers and everything else, mum was always there. Even if there was anything going on in school, like a fun day, mum would always come to help out, and always did it with a big smile on her face. back then I do not think mum and dad really knew what I would go on to achieve for myself, but with both mum and dad and all my family supporting me 100% of course, I couldn't fail. They are amazing parents and I have an amazing family.

School Years

When I look back on my childhood school days, I remember them as being some of the happiest days of my life. I went to a great school for children with different types of disabilities; from physical disabilities like mine, to students who had intellectual disabilities. I started school aged three and I was there right up until I was eighteen. I think because the school had lots of children who had various types of disabilities, the school curriculum and teaching methods was somewhat different from what you might call 'normal school'. We had English, Maths, History and Geography, for those of us who could understand those subjects, among other subjects, yet, because of my difficulty with using a pen I would always need someone sitting with me, they are known now as SNA's.

We had things like, physiotherapy, swimming, wheelchair football and wheelchair basketball every week. I liked all the sports we did in school because we were all mixing and making great friends, don't get me wrong, I loved school but there were hard times for me to.

Thinking back now, to when I was younger, I must have had eight or nine different operations on both legs at different times throughout my early life. The operations were to help my leg muscles loosen, thus enabling me to walk a little, or at the least be able to stand up. I also underwent these procedures to enable me to get myself in and out of my wheelchair with a little assistance. Thanks to years of hard work from myself, and the love and encouragement from my mum and dad, we got there. I can take a few steps and get in and out of the wheelchair, with a little help.

Unfortunately, with operations you got lots of time off school and it was like that for everyone who went to my school. It was assumed that anyone attending my school would never be capable of completing the Junior Cert, this was unacceptable; so the students from the year before me and my own year students wanted to do these exams. I those in my year sat our teachers down and asked them to help us to do our exams. The teachers agreed and over our last two years of being in school, all of my class completed three subjects in the Junior Cert, and I past them all with A's. So proud of that achievement.

Then came the time for me to leave school. Like any teenager I could not wait to leave and move on with my life. I had so many ideas of what I wanted to do with my life and at the very top of my list was to work in radio or T.V. I will always remember this one day, a few months before leaving school, myself and the other students in my year and our parents had this big meeting with the teachers from our school and managers from adult day centres. They thought we would all want to go to one of these centres when we finished school. Now, I am not knocking Adult Day Centre's, I understand there are people who need or want to spend their days at such centres, but from day one I told everyone that I would not be going anywhere near a Day Centre. I told both mum and dad, "I'll stay at home before I ever go to one". Mum did manage to talk me around to talking with a manager of a Day Centre, just to see what they had on offer. I think we spent all of five minutes with the manager and I turned to my mum and said, "No mum, this place isn't for me, we are going". So we left and I have never looked back.

Stepping Out into the Real World

I remember my mum sitting me down one day and telling me the story of when she knew that her little girl was all grown up. I was aged around thirteen when it was decided by the school that I was old enough to bring my powered wheelchair home.

Mum said the day I came home in it was when she realised I had gained my own independence, and yes, she was right. For myself though, I would say it was when I left school for good.

About six months following this, a friend told me about a place in Bluebell where the staff there helped people who had disabilities look for paid work, so I e-mailed them for an appointment and got myself a Jobcoach Assistant. Within three weeks I had my very first interview for a C.E. Programme with the Ballyfermot Theatre Workshops (B.T.W.). The job was learning, working and acting in theatrical drama. I loved every minute of it, even though it brought with it its own set of challenges.

There was forty of us all together on the C.E. Programme. Three wheelchair users, some unmarried mothers and everyone else who worked there had suffered with addiction in their lives or were just unemployed. I do remember my mum asking me, "Are you sure you want to do this C.E. Programme, Lorraine"? To which I always replied, "Yes mum; of course I do, it's a paid job".

I worked with Robbie Healy and Gerry Royal and all the guys at the B.T.W. for three very happy years and we all felt like one big family. It was while working in the B.T.W. that Robbie discovered I wanted to start volunteering in radio and he told me about the radio station, West Dublin Access Radio (WDAR), which was based on the first floor of the Ballyfermot Civic Centre, where we worked, and they had been looking for someone to do a thirty minute, weekly radio show for them.

Robbie took me up to meet them and that is where my radio adventure began. I took on the thirty minute music show, and for five years I was, "DJ Hotwheels". Wonderful.

My Early 20's

Let's skip to the year 2005. I was twenty one in July and I had just finished working with the Ballyfermot Theatre Workshops while still volunteering and doing my radio show every Friday. I needed something else to keep me busy during the week.

I went back to see if I could get a Jobcoach Assistant again to assist me in looking for a new job, but this time it was not so easy finding one. You see, when my Jobcoach Assistant and I went looking to get me onto a new C.E Programme, we were told, "No, sorry, you've already done C.E. before, so you can't go on C.E. again; but come back to us in three years and you can re-apply for a new C.E. Programme".

I was starting to feel very down in myself. I was meeting my Jobcoach Assistant every week and applying for lots of jobs but I was getting nothing back. By that September, my Jobcoach Assistant asked if I would go and talk to the lovely people at the National Learning Network, to see if I could do a course and add it to my Curriculum Vita. I agreed and so we called them and made an appointment for the following week.

I went along with an open mind not really knowing what to expect. I met with two different teachers from two different courses. They were both really nice and they both seemed really interested in what I wanted for myself from my time there. I told them all about my dreams of being able to get a paid job working in radio or T.V. and they both told me, "don't worry. One of us will help you get to where you want to be". An hour later I got a call to say that, because I knew exactly what field I wanted to work in, they thought the best course for me would be the six month back to work course, they offered me a place straight away and I started with them two weeks later.

Even though I had everything in place, like my Personal Assistants, who would come in with me every day from the Irish Wheelchair Association, they would give me a hand with anything I needed for two hours a day, for the rest of the day I was managing myself in my classroom setting. It quickly became noticeable to both me and the class teacher that I was too intelligent to be doing the work that he was giving everyone else in the class. He realised he needed to set me my own work to gauge if I had the ability of reaching the standard of work needed for college. Within weeks he knew that I could in fact manage the work, so we both went online looking for radio courses that I could apply for.

We found two radio courses. A one year Beginner's Course in Radio and a Higher National Diploma (HND) in Radio. We then called Ballyfermot College of Further Education (BCFE) to arrange a meeting to talk over my options with them. They were very helpful and invited me to call in and see them the following week and talk through everything with them. On the day of the meeting at the college I was very nervous so I asked my teacher to coming along to the college with me, 'just for support'.

When we got there we met with both Mr. Tom Conway, Year Head of the one year Radio Beginners Course, and Mr. Simon Maher (no relation), the head of the two year Higher National Diploma in Radio. After talking with both of them for a time, they both left me for what seemed like an age and then came back only to tell me, "unfortunately we don't think we are going to be running our one year Radio Course this year, because we have not got enough people interested in it". It wasn't looking good; but then they told me, "However, we would love to offer you a place on the Higher National Diploma Radio Course". They also told me that I would be teaching them something too, as I would be the very first wheelchair user to attend any course within Ballyfermot College of Further Education (BCFE). They informed me that, given my disability, they could offer me extra time to complete the course, so instead of it taking the standard two years, I could finish it in five years. Anyone who has any kind of disability can ask for this option. Not one for breaking with tradition, I decided I would do it in the three years.

College Life

I look back with great fondness at the wonderful memories and fantastic experiences of my college life. Although traditionally everyone's first year in college would normally begin in September, mine began in the last week of August.

Simon Maher (no relation), was the Year Head for year one students studying the Two Year HND Radio Course I applied for and was accepted onto. I remember one day, Simon called me to ask if I would mind coming in to the college. They wanted to guarantee they had everything ready for me as I was due to start with them the following week. I was informed also that I would be introduced to the Disability Officer, whose job is to support people with Disabilities, like myself and assist us with integrating into the college setting. So of course I went in and I was feeling very excited but very nervous at the same time, not really believing that this was happening for me, to me.

On the day of the meeting with Simon, he walked me around all of the college's new and old buildings; showing me all the classrooms that I would be in. I do believe myself, Simon Maher and Bernard Evans, the Year Head for year two of the course, and a tutor I would be taking some of my subjects with in year one, were all collectively hoping and praying, as we all walked around, that my wheelchair would fit into all classrooms and especially the two on-site radio studios that we would be using every day. Some classrooms where small, yes and both Simon and Bernard needed to change the radio studio around, just a bit, to enable my wheelchair to get in behind and out from behind the radio desk, "No worries Lorraine, we'll sort everything before you start on Monday. We'll see you then".

It was now time for me to meet with the Disability Officer for the college. She informed me of everything that I would be entitled to get for free while I was doing any course within BCFE, or any other college for that matter. She said that I am entitled to attend their college, and that her job, while I was there, was to help me access anything that I might need throughout my time in college and help me out she did, be it filling out grant application forms, or even seeking financial assistance with transportation in order to get me to and from college every day. She also assisted me with getting a note taker who came with me to every lecture to take all my notes electronically. Also, she arranged for me to have my own laptop which was lent to me by the college and included all the software I needed to help me complete all my courses that I would go on to do.

I have to say, I loved the time that I spent on the HND Radio Course. Although it was a huge change for me, being in a classroom setting with 30+ people and even moving classrooms every hour, which at the start was very strange, as I never had that experience when I was in school as a child. I got to experience a lot, such as running an FM radio station in my first year, to running an online station in the second year, there was also work experience involved to.

I completed the HND course in three years with a Distinction Profile. I also went on to complete my Media Management Degree also in BCFE and then went on to do my HND course in Business, also in BCFE. I spent five happy years learning and making some of the very best friends a girl could ever ask for.

Conclusion

If I could say one thing to anyone who is reading this chapter, then it would be this; no matter what happens in life always follow your dreams, because with a little hard work, you too can make anything happen for yourself. I am now working in my dream job as a Freelance Radio Producer, and I am loving life.

Chapter 4

- Love -

By Alan Fay

"The word Love has many variations of meaning; we can love ourselves, we can love our families, we can love an individual as a friend, we can love somebody who we are in a relationship with, and we can even love a sports team. Even broader than the definition of love however; is the varying ways by which it can be expressed"
– Alan Fay

Introduction

Hello, my name is Alan Fay and I am 23 years old. I have one sister and two amazing grandparents. I am a disabled advocate from Dublin Ireland, and I have cerebral palsy. My interests include football, current affairs, and speaking up for and on behalf of people with disabilities. I have my own page on Facebook called 'Life with a Disability'' which I use to advocate for other people living with a disability.

I started this page in 2016 at the age of 19. I use the page as a means of communicating with the community about any problems that I am faced with in society, or any unnecessary obstacles that I may face whilst out in the world such as potholes on the footpaths etc. I do this to provide more awareness of these issues faced by both I and others in a similar situation as myself. This is one of my life passions.

School Life

I attended a local mainstream school until the age of 20 which was called Trinity Comprehensive in Ballymun Dublin. During my time in this school I feel that I was very lucky in the fact that my fellow students were all kind and considerate towards me. They would open doors and make sure that I had whatever I needed. The staff were equally supportive too.

As I approached 20 years of age and was about to leave the school I was asked what it was that I wished to do after completion of secondary. I had always had a keen interest in media, so my answer to this question was simply "Media". Prior to my leaving, the supportive staff within the school tried to find a wheelchair accessible college for me, and also one that could provide me with my required needs i.e. a Special Needs Assistant (SNA).

Ultimately however, despite all the efforts made, I could not get into any college of interest due to lack of funding, combined with the unavailability of an SNA. This was communicated to me by both my secondary school where I was due to leave and the college that I was applying. One such college which informed me that they were inaccessible to my needs, however I know a few individuals who attended that same college and have disabilities, but to me it is 'water off a ducks back' now at this stage.

IWA

I am now a member of the IWA and attend their centre in Clontarf since leaving school. While there I study many different subjects which are all aimed as primary life skills including QQI level 3 qualifications in subjects such as computers, cookery, maths etc. I love going to the IWA as it gives me an incentive to continue meeting and interacting with new people, which I love. It also allows me to meet up with my friends. Without the IWA I honestly do not know where I would be due to my difficulties getting into college. Also, I get a lot of satisfaction from going to the IWA because it gives me the freedom to express myself surrounded by other people with disabilities.

Advocacy

Aside from my social media advocacy work I also go to schools and give talks to able bodied students about the importance of accepting people with different abilities and not to treat them differently. I have done these types of talks in my old secondary school a number of times while also providing this service to other mainstream schools with the assistance of the disability support worker in the IWA. I have been doing this with another member for the past year or so. To date I have done a number talks with the IWA, the first of which was September 2019.

During these talks I highlight the importance of accepting a disabled person as being capable of achieving a lot of the same things as the students, and not to presume from first glance that a disabled person is any different to themselves. Also, there are hidden disabilities that must be compassionately and not sympathetically considered too. One of the most important messages that I try to get across to these students is that although there are a large variety of disabilities which can prevent a person's ability to verbally communicate, this does not mean that that individual is incapable of communicating an alternative way, and the students must do their utmost to allow the disabled individual to communicate via whatever means they feel comfortable with.

In cases where there are extreme physical difficulties such as severe cerebral palsy then this can be achieved by reading the disabled individuals facial expressions to get an indication. My new role of advocating for the disabled within mainstream schools combined with my social media page have both added to my sense of purpose, which I love.

I feel somewhat obligated, but equally proud of being able to do this advocacy, and as I have already stated, this is my passion. This passion is best defined with the reasoning behind why I do what I do. First and foremost, this because I have a disability myself and the work that I am doing is assisting me personally. Secondly, I am advocating because I want to be a better person, who provides to ALL people with disabilities both generosity from myself, and understanding from the able bodied majority who share this world with us

One Love

In 1990 Manchester based band "The Stone Roses" released a song called "One Love". This song is symbolic to a certain football team as the phrase "One Love" is used by the fans of that team. The phrase can be seen on t-shirts sold in the clubs fan store which is located within its stadium. It can also be seen on banners around the stands of its stadium.

This stadium is commonly known globally as Old Trafford, it is known by its fan base as "The Theatre of Dreams"....and the team to which it houses is Manchester United...my "One Love".

I have supported the "Red Devils" for as long as I can remember, and this love was greatly influenced by my friends and certain members of my family, in particular my Father and Uncle. I have been to this stadium roughly four times, the first of which was when I was aged 16. I have travelled a few times to Old Trafford with a supporters club that I use to be part of and also my Father and Uncle.

 One of the most amazing moments that I remember witnessing in Old Trafford was against Aston Villa in which Robin Van Persie scored one of his many amazing volleys.

Even though I love supporting United, and I love going over to Old Trafford to see them play, it can at times be very frustrating for me that I live in Ireland and cannot see them play as often as I would like, or meet some of my favourite players in person. Also, it is frustrating to be unable to actually obtain a ticket for a match in the first place. This can be more difficult for me as opposed to most other supporters given the fact that I am in a wheelchair. However, the moments that I have been able to visit the Theatre of Dreams, I have loved every second.

The Importance of Self-Love

I would like you the reader of this book to ask yourself this question, how do you feel when you receive a letter or card from another person and within that card they are indicating to you how they are thinking about you, in a good way? Would I be correct in assuming that the answer to this question is that you feel loved by that individual? Well, let us peel back the onion a bit here. When you feel loved off that person does it also make you, even if by just a small amount, love yourself due to being loved by another?

The fact that an individual went out of their way to firstly purchase a card, fill it in, and then post it to you should fill you with a sense of self love, and self love is important.

 I love myself, I Alan Fay, love Alan Fay. Why? Because I KNOW for a FACT that I am loved by others, I know that I am in the thoughts of others, and I also know that I have an AMAZING attitude towards life, considering all of the obstacles that I face on a daily basis. I realise that this is a unique mindset to have, as I am fully aware that there are a large amount of people out there who do not love others, and do not love themselves. There are also people out there who show an absolute lack of respect for not only other people, but their own bodies too. This is both selfish and unloving of the miracle that they are for even being given life. It is important to love not only other people, but you too, this is vital in my opinion.

Do not get me wrong, I do get moments where I feel down and dejected, but I ALWAYS attempt and then succeed at bringing my mind back to a more grounded, positive and loving mindset. I feel that I am able to achieve this due to the fact that I have always been surrounded by a loving, kind, supportive and respecting family.

Conclusion

In conclusion, although love has many definitions while also having many ways of being expressed, in my opinion it all boils down to one thing...

Find something you are passionate about, be it a sporting team, be it a career path, be it a group of close friends, or be it another individual; and prepare to fight hard to demonstrate your passion...on a daily basis. This is how you can love both yourself, and the external world around you.

Chapter 5

- Imagination -

By Michelle Rooney

"If we had no imagination we would not be able to achieve anything that we wanted to achieve within our lives...for this reason it is very important to have and use our imaginations...they are what keep us going"
– Michelle Rooney

Introduction

My name is Michelle Rooney; I am a 30 year old woman from Dublin in Ireland. I have a loving and supportive family and plenty of great friends. I am a successful business owner running my own clothes shop in the local shopping centre since leaving school....that last part was a distortion of the truth, but is a long lasting vision of mine which I have been imagining for years. So, why mention it you may ask? I mention it not out of deceit....but merely to demonstrate to you the sheer power of imagination, and its ability to release us from our existing truths and to highlight that however good our lives currently are; we will always imagine something better for ourselves.

My name is Michelle Rooney, I am really a 30 year old woman from Dublin in Ireland who does have a loving and supportive family; with plenty of great friends, and this is all true. Another truth is this, I have always desired to run my own clothes shop but as of yet am limited to only living that part within my imagination. You see, I was born with a disability known as Cerebral Palsy which although not affecting my ability to walk and talk, does affect my ability to do other things no matter how much I long for them. Also, I have photosensitive Epilepsy which affected me badly when I was younger, but thankfully I have not had a seizure within the past two years, which I am delighted with. I attended a school for people with physical disabilities, and this was conveniently located around the corner from my family home. I made a lot of friends while in this school and am thankful to each one for their lasting friendships. I have always had a loving and supportive family around me my entire life, and I wish to take this opportunity to thank them also. Since leaving school at the age of 18 I have not had the same opportunities as most, due to this I have not yet had the opportunity of seeking out my imagined visions for my life. I have only had the ability to live my life the way I have been, a life that I love, but a life with parts missing, and those parts reside within my imagination, where I love to escape to, every now and then.

Early life

From the age of four to eighteen I attended Scoil Mochua, which as I have stated above is a school for people with physical disabilities. During my fourteen years within that school I spent the first half of my time there struggling with the work that I was being given by my teachers. I found certain subjects very difficult and not to my liking or interest such as maths. I would often find myself drifting off into a daydream during classes as I had a lack of interest in what was being taught to me, and this would cause me great difficulties with concentrating. One subject that I had particular interest in however was computers; this was made more interesting to me by the individual who was teaching it, her name is Lorraine Keogh. I can honestly say that without Lorraine Keogh's ability to teach me computers in the way she did, I would not be able to do all that I can do today. Among other teachers who helped me greatly during my time in that school I wish to give a special mention to two sisters who were both my teachers at certain stages, these are Fionnuala and Moira.

School can be difficult for most children, disabled or not, but for me the difficulties that I experienced at times were made all that much easier thanks to the peers I was surrounded with on a daily basis. Scoil Mochua is not the same as mainstream schools within Ireland, and this is for two reasons.

Firstly, it is primarily for children with physical disabilities and secondly it only has a small amount of students to cater for. When I was there the number of students was somewhere between 90-100.if even that. Due to this we were all friends, with most students forming close friendships with an individual or group of individuals, and some of those friendships lasting beyond our schooling years and well into adulthood. I have one such friend, Melissa Tuohy.

While I was a young teenager in Scoil Mochua I took part in some recreational therapy which was organised and overseen by the schools onsite physiotherapist. I found this to be great fun and really liked being around the horses as I visualized myself working with horses when I grew up, and this made me happy and excited.

Although difficult at times my school years within Scoil Mochua were also full of fun, laughter, and the forming of lasting friendships. I thanked the heavens that I was blessed with such a powerful imagination as I have because this got me through some difficult times while in school. The ability to visualise yourself in a more comfortable situation, whether it's in the present time or thinking about the future should never be underestimated. When I reached 18 years of age it was time for me to leave the school and take with me all the knowledge that I had learnt about boring things such as maths and history, important things such as how to make and keep friendships, and lastly my imagination which had proven to be my most powerful tool.

Post School

As I left Scoil Mochua and braced myself for the 'big bad world' of adulthood I left with a FETAC level three in Cookery skills which I obtained in the school at age 16. Due to the lack of opportunities elsewhere I attended an Adult Education Centre in Lucan known as Rossecourt Resource Centre which provides numerous services to attendees all aimed at equipping an individual with the required skills to progress into higher education.

 Making a transition in life can be difficult for anyone; it can be more difficult if you have been attending the same place for as long as I was in Scoil Mochua. Thankfully however some of my friends from school were in Rossecourt too, this made such a huge transition that bit easier for me to handle.

In total I spent four years in Rossecourt learning many various skills such as hairdressing, woodwork, sewing, and cutlery preparation in the canteen.

At the age of 22 I left Rossecourt and attended another centre called 'Seeds' which to my recollection was based in or around Walkinstown in Dublin. While there I expanded my computer skills further from what I had done in Scoil Mochua. I attended that centre for one year and I then moved to the National Learning Network where I presently am based.

At this centre I have learned some additional skills and am now working within the local community one day a week. I work in a Down Syndrome Ireland charity shop in Clondalkin village. My role while working there is primarily to fix up the clothes and other stock that is sold by the shop. I do this type of work every Tuesday for two hours. A few of the days during the week I will also meet up with my key worker. I really enjoy working in the charity shop, and meeting with my key worker too, but I love nothing more than going out in the beautiful environment on walks, and reading books of which I have plenty. I love books, I love reading a variety of different types of books because they fill my mind with fantastic imagined images of things that I would love to do, things that I believe that I can and will eventually do, and things that are best done, and only truly possible, in the amazing world of my imagination.

Protection from Above

I would just like to say before going into further detail that I am a believer, what I mean by that is I am religious and have a firm belief in the fact that every single person on this planet has a guardian angel. I have believed this for as long as I can remember.

During my moments of feeling sad and alone I will often have to remind myself that "I am protected, my guardian angel has my back and will look after me". I tell myself this even after my belief has been rejected or laughed at by others.

This belief is important to me in particular and relates so much to the message within this chapter, here is why:

If I believe that I am unable to do certain things within my life given my disability, and other people are confirming those 'restrictions' to me every now and again, then my only form of escape is my imagination, which can be a lonely place to be at times, but knowing that my guardian angel is there with me, watching over me in my real and physical life, and watching over me in my imagined life too, then I am NEVER ALONE. This piece of knowledge is so important to me and for me too.

Conclusion

Ever since I was younger there are lots of places I imagined that I would love to go. I never knew about many places in the world until people began talking about them. I would find these places very interesting and always ask what the places were like.

There are a few places I would LOVE to travel to such as Jamaica, China, Japan, and England. I would also love to visit California and Hawaii in the USA as well as Disney World Florida. I always imagined what it would be like to visit these places and to have experiences that I would never forget.

I will just have to live with these visions of myself travelling to these places in my imagination for now. I will visit them one day though. I believe that much, and in my opinion belief is all we need. Belief in ourselves firstly, and belief in the possibilities as to what we are capable of achieving. It is important to respect one another but it is more important to respect yourself, respect your dreams, respect your fantasies, and respect all that you are.

It is perfectly fine in my opinion, to be a little bit selfish every now and again, there is nothing wrong with looking after number one. I know that for me personally I have to stop being so concerned about what is going on around me, things that I can do nothing about, and things that do not concern me in the first place. This is why, as I have said previously, if there is nothing you can do about a situation on the outside of your mind, then revert to the inside of your mind and imagine the wondrous positive possibilities that you CAN control. To me, this is not only important; it is the best way to deal with the negative situations that sometimes come into my own life.

In relation to my fantasies of travelling the world, even if I never do all of this, even if I just have to continue living with these imagined visions of myself travelling the world, even if that is all that I can do due to my restrictive way of life, I am happy.

I am happy because I KNOW for a fact that I have a kind loving and supporting family around me, I KNOW that I have an amazing network of friends around me, and lastly and most importantly in my opinion I KNOW that whenever life gets me down, or becomes too much to handle, I can always escape even if just temporarily, to the world of my imagination.

EMPOWERING ABILITIES

- Voices of the Voiceless –

Chapter 6

- Tenacity -

By Paul Gantley

"Do not allow your adversities to own you.
Instead, show tenacity and rise above"
– Paul Gantley

Introduction

My name is Paul Gantley; I was born on the 23rd October 1979 in the Lourdes hospital Drogheda. My Dad's and Mother's names are Mick and Carmel Gantley. I live in a beautiful house 4 1/2 miles outside Drogheda. I live with my Dad, my sister Mary, my nephew Christopher and my 3 huskies Crystal, Bailey, and Titan A.K.A. 'The Boss'.

When I was a child my Mother and I were always 'Partners in Crime'; and wherever she went I would go also. Many a cold winters morning during my Mother would ask me "Is it too cold to go to school today?" to which I would obviously reply "Yes" and my both my Mother and I would then head off down to my Granny Reagan's, Uncle Michael, Uncle Paddy, Uncle Tom and Uncle 'Dermys' house.

When we got there my Granny would say to me "so it's too cold to go to school, but it's not too cold to come to see me" as she rubbed her chin with a cheeky grin ha. While there we would sing, tell stories and jokes during the day; and play cards at night. I have very happy memories with them all and they helped shape the person who I am today.

My Granny died on the 30th of September 1992, she was 91 years old, just short of her 92nd birthday, which would have been on the 14th of January.

My Mother sadly passed away from Breast Cancer on the 20th of January 1996 at the age of 56; and this I took very badly. After her passing I would not get out of bed or eat properly for two years until one day I came to the eventual realisation; which hit me like a ton of bricks. The disbelief I experienced as I thought about the fact that I cannot see her anymore was heartbreaking to me; but I knew that I would and will always remain knowing; that she is still with me.

Tenaciously fighting on: With the Power of Music

From an early age I have always had a love for music. My sister Mary is a classically trained pianist. During my youth; I was in awe of the music that she was so seemingly effortlessly and beautifully capable of playing.

Through listening to Mary playing I was so inspired that I got my own keyboard. One day I was listening to the radio and a Joe Dolan song "It's you, it's you, it's you" came on and I began playing. My Dad came into the room thinking that it was the radio and could not believe that it was me. In that moment I discovered a previously hidden gift; I could play a song without reading the music. I am now self thought in the piano and can play different forms of music through firstly listening to it; and then subsequently playing that piece of music myself. I am very much aware and proud of the fact that this form of art skill is as unique as I am as an individual. Also, I had previously learnt the Violin from the early age of 9.

I took it upon myself to sit exams in the field of Violin playing and delightfully went on to pass all 8 of them with honours.

After my Mothers passing I could not concentrate properly on my school work as I was overwhelmed with grief and shock, I ultimately left school, I was 16 at the time. I went on to get a job in 'The Sound Shop' in Drogheda where I worked for 17 years.

While there I had many various roles within my day-to-day work life. Initially, my job title was a 'Trained Sales Assistant' which required me to primarily 'keep an eye' on the phones dealing with general queries from customers calling in and I would also demonstrate the keyboards to potential customers if needed.

One day which stands out in my memory in particular a man came into the shop with a CD. He asked if there were anyone who could teach him one of the songs on it.

That store did provide lessons but these were unfortunately all booked up at the time. I asked the man "let me to hear the song and I will see if I can pick the chords out myself". He picked up a guitar from within the shop and between him and I we both listened intently to the song in question. Within a matter of five minutes he was able to play this song. The song was an American folk song which I forget the name of; and the artist too it was that long ago to be honest. But, I know that I had never heard the song before that day.

One of the funniest roles I ever had while working in that shop was as the store security. One story which stands out in my mind primarily for its pure funniness is when one of my sisters friends turned to her and said "Mary, have you been down in the Sound Shop recently" to which my sister replied "No, Why?" "Because I was down there the other day having a look around and this fella in a wheelchair was there watching everything the whole time, and you wouldn't be able to get past him if you tried! Whoever he was!" to which Mary replied "That's my brother"

From the Shadows of Grief, a Song is Born

During my youth I had written a few small insignificant songs; one of which was on the Violin at the age of 9 or 10.

However, one day during my two years of heartbreak and shock at what had happened to my Mother, I manoeuvred myself towards my keyboard with the initial intention of just playing some covers of already existing and well known songs. During my playing of one such song I inadvertently miss hit a chord and suddenly was inspired by what I had just heard. I then continued on adding variations of keys and my innate creative side took over. Within the space of around 5 minutes I had created my very first full piece of unintentional but meaningful and significant music, and also the lyrics.

Two days later I approached my sister and asked her to have a listen to my new creation. To say that she was blown away by this is nothing more than an understatement as Mary was amazed at what I had just created, so much so that she invited a friend to hear it. Mary's friend Denise ó Rourke who is a singer also loved my song. With both of their encouragement this snow balled both the song and me into the limelight. Both Denise and I recorded this song on my 21st birthday; with Denise providing vocals, which I then submitted to RTE's 'Open House' to see if they were interested in it featuring on the show.

In 2000, thanks in large part to Mary and Denise's astonishing support and belief I appeared on 'Open House' with Denise providing the vocals for this performance while I played on a grand piano. This incredible opportunity allowed me to introduce the world to my song; a song which I called "Without You" and became a tribute to my late Mother.

A number of years later the president of the Spina Bifida Association, a man by the name of Tom Scott asked me if I would play a song on the keyboard at the Spina Bifida 'Shine' week. This is a weeklong annual awareness event run by the association. Without any hesitation I knew exactly what it was that I would play during this performance, my song "Without You". On the day as soon as I had finished playing this song I delightfully discovered that Tom had recorded my playing on his phone. I asked him to send me the recording which he did on Instagram messenger and I then put it onto my own Instagram feed. I was overwhelmed with shock and disbelief at the amount of support that I was receiving as it got 193 views within a matter of minutes. This then prompted me to also put it up on Facebook; and from there it quickly went viral. To date that video has had over 45,000 views with the original post being shared roughly 150 times around the world.

All of this started from an error that I made on my keyboard and this proved to me that even though mistakes may happen, sometimes magic and inspirational moments may also occur during such supposed mistakes; providing we are listening out for them. I have subsequently gone on to write many more songs, 10 in fact, all of which are due to be included on an album which is due to be released soon.

Protection from Above

Not too long after my appearance on 'Open House' I was rushed to hospital with septicemia which was caused by a bad kidney infection and I was given six hours to live. My sister stormed heaven praying for me and one of my friends who didn't show emotion much rang my sister and was very emotional wondering how I was. Even though I was out of it on morphine to help me deal with the pain I told my Dad that "I'm going into ICU to get better" I firmly believe that with my Mammy, Granny, and Padre Pio with me that I am still here to tell the tale.

I actually had a near death experience during my stay in hospital. I saw my mother wearing a bright blue cardigan in heaven. My sister came into the room wearing the same cardigan and still out of it on morphine I went ballistic "get that cardigan off you, that's mammy's cardigan" I shouted.

Years later I just happened to say I had a near death experience, I saw mammy wearing a blue cardigan in heaven. Mary said "so that's why ya lost it that day" with a laugh.

I have since had a kidney transplant, which took place on the 8th of May 2015. After five years of dialysis which was tough especially while working three days a week, one day I finally got the call that I had been waiting for. They had found a match.

After that procedure, I made a remarkable recovery and was discharged from the hospital within 10 days. The surgeon had said to me that my creatinine was better than hers.

A friendship is born: Lorraine Keane

One day while on social media I decided to send some well-known Irish celebrities friend requests, just to see if they would accept such a request from me. One such celebrity was Lorraine Keane of Xpose. I followed up this request with a message to Lorraine stating "Hi Lorraine, you are one of my favourite TV presenters and I was just wondering if you would accept my friend request? Hope you are well" and much to my surprise Lorraine accepted and replied "Thanks Paul". Since then the two of us have been chatting and met in person four times. In my honest opinion she is a lovely person with a heart of gold who has been very supportive and kind towards me and all I do.

The first time I met Lorraine was when she was judging ladies day at Bellewstown races. We had became great friends and had chatted about her 'furbabies' as she calls them ha, 'Chip and slipper'. I text her one day and said "Hi pal, I see you are doing ladies day at Bellewstown. Would it be OK if I came out to meet you?" to which she replied "Let's do it! And Paul, Don't worry about anything, it's all on me".

I have photos with her from that day too. I also met her lovely family, her husband Peter, and her daughter Romy. I still have to meet her other daughter Emelia someday too, and of course Chip and Slipper ha.

 I organised transport and a P.A. to also make it to Lorraine's fundraising event 'Fashion relief', which is in its third year. She runs this event in Cork, Galway, and Dublin every year. I went to the one in the RDS Dublin last year. Prior to arriving to this my sister said to me "now Paul, don't be disappointed if Lorraine hasn't much time to talk to you. She'll be very busy" to which I replied "Ah yeah sure I know that, but it will be nice to see her and support her". When I went up to the stage and called her name she could not see me, but when she did she dropped what she was doing and came over to me and gave me the biggest hug. She was so thankful that I made the effort to get up to her event. The event is ran in aid of the third world, and anyone with 'pre-loved' clothes can donate them to fashion relief, check them out on Instagram.

 Becky and Danni were there too, all were only too delighted to see me and make time for a chat. Check out Facepainters Dublin, Beck Keane make up. Tori Keane hair. Good people like those deserve all the support in the world. I was coming home from a hospital appointment one day and I heard Lorraine's husband Peter on the Radio, and I text her and said "I heard Peter on the radio" and she text back "Yep he was on today, he's on tomorrow too. I'll get him to play a song for you.

My own song had gone viral at this stage, so she picked 'Big time' by Peter Gabriel, I detect devilment in that selection ha, great tune though.

Through meeting and getting to know Lorraine, I genuinely believe that society has this misguided perception of celebrities as being people who are egotistical and self-centred whereas the reality is in many cases, that even though all that they have achieved in life, celebrities like my pal Lorraine, are just like you or I. They are kind people who just love a chat, and to give and be loved. Pamela Flood, Theresa Lowe, Siobhán Ryan, Flo McSweeney and Evelyn Cusack are lovely people too. I have met Celia Holman Lee at the Curragh too, and one of the models from her agency Elizabeth Mangan sent me a card for my 40th. I met Pamela Flood once at the IWA fashion show and she went out of her way to help others, and even met me afterwards for a chat. This misperception is similar to that as the one attached to people of disability, be it physical or mental.

The perception of a disabled person is that we are in constant need of support and assistance, and that we can do nothing for ourselves. However, this book alone, written by mainly people with physical disabilities during a time of global crisis and fear, proves the contrary. In my opinion, the biggest and most dangerous disabilities that exist within our world are our perceptions.

Conclusion: Tenacity in the Face of Adversity

Although Spina Bifida has its challenges, there are many challenges within life in general, regardless if you are disabled or otherwise. But from my personal perspective as a person living with a disability such as Spina Bifida I will say this: Even though it may not be as easy for me to do the same things as an able bodied person, I feel that it has always been important for me to show true desire and true tenacity to keep going, keep moving forwards in my life. I believe that this and this alone will get me to where ultimately I want to go. The same applies to you the reader.

Equally as important as this however is surrounding yourself with love and kindness, which we all rely on having to get us true this sometimes difficult, sometimes utterly heartbreaking, but other times adventurous and exiting thing called life. I have been blessed with a loving and caring family and equally loving and caring friends. Some of those people who have been there providing me with love, support and encouragement in particular with my upcoming album I now wish to mention within this chapter: My sister Mary Gantley for helping me with the vocals, and within my life in general. My supportive friends who assisted with the production of this album, which was recorded in Abbey Lane Studios...in Drogheda (so not the same one the Beatles came out of ha ☺). Thanks to Fran McDermott on drums, Eric Sharpe on guitar while also Co-Producing and Darren Rooney on bass.

All of these loving and supportive people whom I have in my life have helped me along; and if I combine that with my *positive and tenacious mindset*, I can achieve many things; as can you.

"Without You"

By Paul Gantley

First verse

Here I am on my own wondering what went wrong

I had you now you're gone my life's not the same

people say that I'm crazy but I love...

Chorus

I want you in my life just like it used to be without you I don't know if

I can go on..

Second verse

I wake up every day wonderin where you are

Are you alone like me or is there someone new

People say that I'm crazy but I love you I still love

Repeat chorus

EMPOWERING ABILITIES

- Voices of the Voiceless –

Chapter 7

Note: The following chapter was transcribed and structured by Patrick Hogan. All of which was carried out with the permission of Emer Concannon.

The transcription was created from an agreed recording of a 'Face time' conversation between Emer Concannon, Tracey Mccann and Patrick Hogan held on the 18/04/2020.

- Identity -

By Emer Concannon

"I like to help people who require assistance,
while the rest of the world may simply stare.
This is because; I know exactly how that feels" – Emer Concannon

Introduction

Hello, my name is Emer Concannon and I am from Galway in Ireland. I have a question for you, have you ever heard the saying "Live each day as if it were your last" Well, in my case, to a certain extent, I am forced to flip that age old saying on its head. What do I mean by that you may ask? What I mean is that I, in truth, am forced through no fault of my own; to live each day, as if it were my first, allow me to elaborate.

If our paths were ever to cross, I am certain I would meet a nice, friendly and considerate person, as would you I can assure you. We may exchange pleasantries or talk about mundane things such as the weather and then be on our separate ways. We both may find ourselves thinking "that person was nice". If our paths were to cross again, in let's say a week's time or even less, you would immediately recognize my face and may even remember the impression I gave you the last time we briefly spoke. As for I on the other hand, this would sadly be... my first time meeting you....

My name is Emer Concannon; I live in Galway Ireland, living each day as if it were my first, because in truth, and to an extent, it is...

Imagine that you are a young woman in her early 20's, you are in the process of becoming aware of whom you are as an individual and where you fit within society. You are due to get married to a man who you deeply love, and who loves you in return. All appears to be going to plan in your little world when all of a sudden...seemingly out of nowhere...BANG....you awake in a hospital bed confused as to how you got there, with a strange man sitting beside your bed. The man explains that he is your soon-to-be husband but you do not recollect ever knowing him, and you begin explaining to him that you already have a boyfriend.

However, unbeknown to you, that person whom you assumed was your boyfriend...is no longer part of your life anymore, and has not been for a number of years. The man sitting beside your bed claiming to be your soon-to-be your husband is in fact telling the truth...you just cannot remember.

My name is Emer Concannon; I live in Galway Ireland and this is my story of how 16 years ago I lost my ability to create new, lasting and meaningful short-term memories. This begs yet another question: How can you be expected to truly know who you are today, and who you plan on becoming tomorrow, if you cannot remember who you were yesterday.

My Story

I do not remember the story of how my life changed so drastically, but I know it through others telling me initially, and then by me repetitively reminding myself every single day since.

The story goes that on that day as I was sitting watching television, I suddenly lost the power on one side of my body. I was brought to a hospital on a Sunday night and the power came back on Monday. That Wednesday they performed a Lumbar Puncture and I had a headache afterwards.

I was told that this was ok. On Holy Friday (Good Friday) my brain ruptured causing me to go into a coma. I awoke from that coma on the Monday with no recollection of why I was in the hospital, or who anyone was, including my fiancé.

At the time the Doctors did not know what had caused any of these symptoms that I was experiencing. A few days later they discovered that the cause to this was in fact a rare virus known as 'Hashimoto's Encephalitis' which was effectively attacking my brain, and due to the rarity of this virus it was difficult to diagnose. I spent the following six weeks in hospital and when I was discharged I came out with a scar on a part of my brain known as the temporal lobe consequently affecting my short term memory. I spent the following years attempting to retrain myself to do everything, and most importantly, remembering how to do them.

 One of the affects to my new condition was that I could only remember certain things that were retained within my long term memory, such as family. As I have indicated at the beginning of this chapter, my fiancé was not one of those memories. My fiancé and I's marriage broke up around a year later; this was because, after all, you need a memory in order to fall in love. If your memories of how you feel about a certain individual will not store in your short term memory then it will be harder for them to go into your long term memory. In order for me to fall in love I would require a man with a lot of patience to give me the time required to fall in love with him. The problem with short term memory loss is that you can awake today not knowing how you felt two days ago.

Memory Tools
(Remembering To Remember)

Over the years I have developed methods and used existed 'tools' to assist me with living as much of a normal life as possible. These methods and tools include my social media account (which is always a new experience for me) and also my diary. I write a page within my diary each day. I write in this every night about what happened on that day while looking back over the last few days to establish what happened in my life and what I experienced. The issue that arises from this is that I am dealing with those experiences and the feelings they invoke on a daily basis.

One such entry in my diary was that I have recently been to see a neurologist who informed me that my memory banks were shrinking which I noted had upset me a lot when I was informed of this. I remember this, not only due to my diary entries but also because I am thinking of this fact every single day meaning that I am forcing this memory from my short term memory to my long term memory.

An example of how this works is this, if I were to go to a funeral of a local man let's say a month ago and DID NOT either write this in my diary or force myself daily to remember.

I could then meet that man's wife tomorrow and innocently ask her in friendly chit chat "how is your husband?" to which she may laugh thinking that I am joking and reply "sure weren't you at the funeral? We dropped you home." This would then make me feel like an idiot.

How It Makes Me Feel

I remember when I was a young child who was brought up with religious rituals such as saying a prayer of grace before each meal, and every day in school prior to eating my lunch I would secretly bless myself. I would always feel that I had to hide this from the other students as to avoid being laughed at. Due to my religious upbringing I have always wondered why God has given me such a heavy cross to carry because I felt that I had already been through enough in life and have continuously questioned why he picked me, what was it that I had done wrong that made him pick me and give me all of this difficulty.

The truth is however, that even though I have my daily routines which I have implanted into my long term memory, such as reading through my diary entries, checking my phone to see who I was in contact with the day previous, and reading my notes of what I was to do on any given day, all of which is helpful for the day-to-day stuff, but remembering how I felt yesterday or last week, is a much more difficult thing to note down, and then remember.

Society

Every morning, after I awake and realise again the full extent of my situation, I am also met with feeling as though I am not part of society, I am alienated and seen as bothersome.

When people see me coming, they do their utmost to avoid me. I have noted in my diary that one day I bumped into a local councillor and lip read him saying to himself "oh fu**" when he saw me approaching because I had previously asked him to request the local council to trim the grass on the sides of the road for me because I needed space to be able to walk on.

I feel as though no one wants to know me because I bring a brain injury with me, and this makes me feel lonely.

On the rare occasions that I do go out for a few social drinks I have to be conscious of two things; firstly, how much I consume and secondly, who I socialise with. I always make it my business to sit beside elderly men who do not know me nor I them, and just talk nonsense with them. I find this to be easier to do as opposed to socialising with other women my own age because the conversations with elderly farmers about sheep and cattle are easier for me to manage than conversations about shoes, handbags or general gossip, all of which I have no recollection or even ability to recollect, thus reminding me that I have this condition.

All the time while I am talking and joking with the farmers by saying things to them such as "I'll marry you and then drop you back to the nursing home" or "I bought these shoes in New York and the next pair you will be buying me because you will be my husband".

Society would say that I am cracked because I am talking this type of nonsense to elderly men in a pub, but I do not care. Yes, it hurts me when people say mean things to me but to be perfectly honest I do not care what they think, all I care about in that moment is making the elderly gentlemen who I am talking to laugh. That makes me happy. When you do not have the ability to store short term memories then it becomes difficult to have the facts of any matter, so all that I am capable of doing while socialising is joking and making others laugh. This is comforting to me due to this fact: society may look down on me and isolate me, and this makes me sad when I do manage to remember situations where I felt this way, and while I agree that everybody out there in the real world has their own problems to deal with, the majority are happy out...whilst I feel left out.

No Bang!

The scarring that I have on my brain left me with another side effect which is that I can become startled very easily and let out a scream "No Bang".

This can be caused by any sudden noise that I may encounter in my day-to-day life, be it the bark of a dog, the beeping of a car horn, the ringing of my door bell or even a noise from my mobile phone, and for this reason I always place my phone on silent.

One story that I know from my diary regarding how this aspect of the brain injury affects me in my day-to-day life is this. One day while I was in the supermarket I had asked the staff to turn off the loud speaker as it was causing me to jump anytime that it went off. I was informed that they would oblige and turn off the loudspeaker. Shortly afterwards however the loudspeaker went off again which caused me to jump and let out a scream. One of the members of staff who was there began laughing and turned away, I did not know his name so I proceeded to take his arm to get his attention and explain to him that my jumping and screaming was caused by a brain injury. I was subsequently barred from the store and have not been allowed enter since due to the stores management claiming that I 'grabbed' a staff member by the arm.

I am bothersome to a lot of people because whenever I go for a walk all dogs must be kept inside due to their barking causing me to jump and scream both uncontrollably and unintentionally. One such dog near where I live has caused these reactions from me a number of times to date. One such incident which took place a few weeks ago was that I reported the owner of that dog to the Gardai because he would not take his dog in for me. I can only remember this because it is in my phone that I rang the local Gardai station but have no recollection as to what the Gardai said to this man. I can only assume that the Gardai called out to the man and informed him to take his dog in but to this day I have noted a few occasions to where this dog was still causing me difficulties while out walking.

My Message

I remember one sentence that was said to me years ago by Fr Oliver Hughes, who was a priest who visited me while I was in the coma, or after I had awoke, I am not too certain, but I remember this sentence and I have thought about it every day since. In the years following my diagnoses of this brain injury I had slowly but surely lost contact with past friends, my finance, and even my family. Society as a whole, treat me like a burden because they do not understand my hidden condition. Fr Hughes on the other hand had not only remained in contact with me and would text me "Goodnight" every evening, making me feel as though I am not on my own and that I have somebody in my life who cares, he also fully understood and could relate to the challenges that I continue to encounter within my life. Fr Hughes was diagnosed with Leukaemia and sadly passed away, prior to his passing however he said to me *"now I know what you have been talking about when you have something that nobody can see"*.

Conclusion

(Identity = Knowing One's Self)

To truly know one's self, one must firstly be aware and have an understanding of the following: One's own emotions, desires, and abilities. For me personally, I do not know how to feel about a situation that I cannot remember as ever occurring. I cannot remember how I felt about a situation yesterday, nor can I guarantee any awareness as to how I will feel tomorrow, all I can do is take it one day at a time.

Prior to my diagnoses my plan was to start my own family and that was my desire. This was a desire that was beginning to take shape before my life was turned upside down. Now, I cannot plan anything, and so again all I can do is take this one day at a time.

I might not have the ability to store short term memories, which can be and is very difficult to live with. But, I do have the ability, for example, to make a group of farmers laugh, and assist local elderly people with their day-to-day things such as crossing the road. In conclusion, what I am capable of doing is demonstrating compassion, understanding and kindness to the best of my ability, while living with my brain injury, ***a condition that nobody can see***; all that I expect in return...is for the same.

EMPOWERING ABILITIES

- Voices of the Voiceless –

Chapter 8

- Equality -

By Sandra Dilon

"The dictionary defines Equality as being
'the state of being equal, especially in status, rights, or opportunities'
The reality is however that while these seeking out in the real world
you will be met with a larger number of inequalities.
This is because to some people...it's just a word"

Introduction

Hi my name Sandra and I am a mum to three amazing children. I was asked about equality and what it means to me, and 20 years ago I would have said equality is generally characterized by the idea that all humans are equal, that all citizens of a state should be accorded the exactly equal rights.

However, 20 years later and following a journey into the world of disability, I now say that the state of being equal in status, rights, and opportunities is merely symbolic!

Beginning my Journey

The reason that I now feel the way that I have stated in the above introduction is due to this: 20 to 23 years ago I lived a blissful life with two of my neuro typical children unaware of the injustices that exist in the world of Disability.

Although disability is as old as the human race the experiences felt by disabled people and the issues that arise for them receives little or no consideration. Why, because they are a marginalised sector within society.

How do I know this to be true, because twenty-two years ago a beautiful young man was born into my family and society labelled him, "high functioning autism" Since then I have had to struggle and fight, being met with dead ends, and or large brick walls, all to try and access support and understanding for him.

However, the biggest hurdle was to come when he became 12 years old and I discovered he had no friendships like his siblings, no outlets to experiment with? No acceptance.

The struggle began again and after months of knocking on doors of the public services and approaching local partnerships I discovered the only alternative was to enter the arena and start up a social skills group for teenagers of 12+.

It was a complex situation because my son had attended a main stream school yet he lived with Asperger syndrome/ADD/Dyspraxia, so I had to try and build a bridge to link the two worlds together.

So, after the initial challenges and fears, the Meeting Place Club was established in 2010 for teenagers 12+.

Meeting Place Club

The Meeting Place Club was the first integrated group in Dublin, and I can actually say maybe in Ireland, because before that people with disability for some reason were put in their own category or boxes which meant that there was no integration and mixing of various disabilities.

 As the years unfolded the never-ending challenges continued with funding and issues associated with mental health. This was because in Ireland you are not allowed have more than one issue when you have a disability.

The demand grew for these injustices to be met with resistance, and teenagers came from all over the city to take part in The Meeting Place Club.

However when you are a voluntary group the process is slow but that has not stopped this club as to date we have helped 300-400 teenagers, and now younger children, because our motto is: ***"if you're different, we don't turn you away"***.

Parents come seeking support, but more importantly a listening ear, just like me. I am someone who all those years ago was just looking for someone who had wore the T-shirt so to speak.

After 10 years of friendship building and teaching self-regulation to the teenagers my thoughts are now looking to ability and adaption.

I am now mindful of the unfairness of my sons' journey and furthermore I can still hear his two siblings asking "why can't our brother travel on the same journey as us".

I can see clearly the discrimination and injustice practices in equal status with my son's rights and opportunities because of his disability so I will continue to enter the arena to voice my opposition, even though I will face criticism.

In my eye's equality will only be achieved when individuals like my son and others can take their rightful place alongside others on an even playing field.

The Meeting place club is only in its infancy and we are living in a post-recession Ireland, however this has had very little impact on my son's future prospects or that of his friends with disabilities.

Conclusion

In conclusion, I as his mother will continue to face service shortfalls and my son will see increased poverty because of lack of opportunities in employment, because exclusion is part of his daily reality.

Unfortunately, there are still ***no signs of change at political and or public levels.***

So, until the words "**_Adapt_**" and "**_Implement_**" are the key words for equality then the Meeting place club and I will continue to use our strength and courage to deliver compassion and understanding in the world of disability and difference.

Note: The following observation was written by Patrick Hogan.

Seeking justice and equality in an unjust and unequal world

"As we can tell from Sandra's story and her message the level of injustice that exists within not only other countries but also Ireland is astonishing given that it is supposedly the 21st century. Yes, Ireland is now more of a liberal and accepting nation as opposed to how it was 20 years ago (or even less), but the inequalities being met by people of disabilities still exists, and this must be met with some form of resistance, or at the very least advocacy...**but this is just my opinion.**

Since 2005 we as a nation have put in place the 'Disability Act 2005' which grants the disabled population of the Republic of Ireland with a right to access public services and facilities. In 2007 Ireland signed 'The UN Convention on the Rights of Persons with Disabilities'.

The purpose of the Convention is to promote, protect and ensure the *full and equal enjoyment of all human rights* and fundamental freedoms by all persons with disabilities, and to promote respect for their inherent dignity. It applies established human rights principles from the UN Declaration on Human Rights to the situation of people with disabilities.

Although agreed to in 2007 by the then Irish Government it took 10 years for this to be ratified by our government, during which time...*a nation...or at least a portion of it...held its breath.*

Chapter 9

- Strength -

By Patrick Hogan

"Strength is not only found in the measurement of what an individual is physically capable of doing....but also what that individual can mentally and emotionally withstand"

Introduction

My name is Patrick Hogan, and I am the strongest person I know. For anyone who has ever met me before, that may seem like a pretty bold statement to make, and for anyone reading this that has not had the pleasure of meeting me; allow me to elaborate. I am a 35 year old disabled citizen of Ireland. Born in 1985 to Eithne and Patrick Hogan Snr; I was not what you would call a "normal" baby. Upon my birth the doctors present noticed something that immediately distinguished me from other newborn babies; I had failed to cry after my grand entrance into the world. They carried out their tests and scans and discovered that my heart and lungs had not developed currently and as such I would not have had enough energy to cry.

This was shocking to my parents at the time; and they worried endlessly about me and my future. Well, my mother did anyway; my father on the other hand disappeared from the scene a few years later as he could not wrap his head around the concept of having a child with a disability; adios pops and good riddance. Thankfully, my dad's family still wanted to be part of mine and my two sisters' lives. Prior to my father 'running for the hills' in Wales where he still lives to this day; at the age of 1, and on my first birthday in fact, I took a stroke. This left me with right-side hemiplegia, which is similar to cerebral palsy and meant that, because of the times i.e. the early 90's, I would have to attend a school for people with physical disabilities. I attended this school from the age of 4 until 18 years old.

One of the things that I have always found most difficult to deal with more than the visibly obvious physical disability is the hidden disability that caused it to happen. I cannot run because of this, I even struggle at times walking up a hill or against wind; my breath is quite literally taken from me which can then exasperate the heart. I was mocked constantly for the way my right arm looked; and called every name in the book I might add. Still though, it's not all bad, my life so far has been full of challenges and obstacles yes; but I have ALWAYS been strong enough to face them. Maybe not physically, but mentally; so what I meant to say at the beginning of this chapter was that I am 'mentally the strongest' person that I know and according to my rulebook, which I have abided by my entire life; that is all that matters.

I would like you now to imagine this scenario, picture a young boy let us say around the age of 8 or 9 who lives in what would be regarded as an under developed suburb within the city of Dublin. This child has many challenges to overcome such as being verbally and sometimes physically attacked by the neighboring children for his glaringly obvious and somewhat differing physical appearance from those of another child his age. In one such scenario this boy had a plastic bottle of his favorite drink snatched from his back pocket and upon pleading for it to be returned to him was instead met with it being forcefully thrown back at him thus causing him to bleed from the point of impact, his head!

That form of abuse can alter a boy in many ways; thankfully however, if it were me, it would have just *made me stronger.*

Acting Strong

Growing up I had no friends aside from school friends; and that of my younger sister's friends. My sister, Lesley-Anne, and I always had a close bond growing up together. My mother always compared us to twins; which was fitting until my mother had actual twins in 1999.

My dependency on Lesley-Anne's friends all changed when I took a brave step forward within my own self. The fact that I was mocked daily by the neighbouring children due to my disability made my family believe that it had greatly affected my confidence.

For the briefest of moments in my youth; it honestly did. This all changed when one day I made a quick decision to do something for myself that even my family were surprised at, even though my mother suggested it to me; I began attending a local drama club.

I vividly remember the night I took this massive plunge into the unknown and scary world of stage acting. My mother, sisters and I were attending a play of the hit musical 'Grease'. This play was being run by a children's drama group called 'Dreamworks'.

The children in the group featured local children from a variety of ages; between the ages of 7 to 17. During the interval of this show my mother turned to me and asked if I was enjoying it so far; to which I enthusiastically replied "Yes". My mother then asked me the question that, in my honest opinion, changed my life. She asked me "would you like to join it?" To which I replied "Yes, but how can I?"

My mother told me to ask the man who runs the group if I could join; his name was Declan Cummins or "Deco". My Mam almost immediately saw him and pointed him out to me; and I shyly approached him. "Sorry, Deco?" I said to this man who I had never spoken to before. "Yeah" He sharply replied. "I was wondering if I could ask you if I could join the drama group?" I asked. "I'll be having auditions in a few weeks time and we can see what you can do" he replied. "What about this?" I asked pointing at my right arm. "What about it?" He replied. "All I care about is if you can act" he said, and then walked off to prepare for the beginning of act two.

I auditioned a few weeks later and was ecstatically informed later that evening that I was successful; this filled me with so much joy for the first time in my life; that I can recollect of.

My first role on the 'grand stage' was in a stage adaptation of Disney's 'Hercules' in which I played a minor role of Hercules adoptive Earth father; a small-time farmer of sorts with plenty of heart and wisdom; rather fitting in my opinion. I embraced this role so much, even though

I was only on stage for the briefest of times. I also had been given, in my opinion, the best line of the show which I told a downhearted and dejected Hercules as he pondered a decision that he felt he must make. This line was "A man's got to do; what a man's got to do"

That always got the audience in hysterics; much to my own amusement, and pride.

It was through this group that I made my first realisation about the strength of a person's character; firstly that of my own, and secondly, that of my mentors; Declan Cummins. What a legend of a man, who I have never had the opportunity to thank for taking a chance on a scrawny disabled boy who just wanted to make friends.

During my time in that drama group I met lots of really nice and welcoming children/adolescents; but the most impactful for me was when I made a friend of my own and not that of my sisters. For the first time in my young life I had a true friend who I am still friends with to this day; Michael Piercy.

Following my 'career' with DreamWorks, I then went onto a company with more of a 'household' name; Dublin Youth Theatre. While there I met a wide variety of characters and people who have made a lasting positive impact on my life.

Three Men and One Wise Lady

There are three men who I wish to acknowledge for teaching me the true value of the words 'inner strength'. The first being my teacher John Maher who as well as my mother thought me the strength of 'knowledge'. Knowledge is a very powerful and strong asset to possess. It is stronger than any weapon ever created by man.

If you do not believe me then ask yourself this, who in your opinion held more eternally lasting strength, the man who conquered nations and killed thousands of his enemies with the swing of his sword; or the man who wrote about him with the swish of his pen? To me the answer is glaringly obvious.

Secondly, Declan Cummins for teaching me the required strength in making the world laugh at me, and being ok with it.

Lastly, John Jordan Snr, for teaching me the most important lesson of all, the strength required in laughing my way through life...as best I can.

Working Hard at Being Strong

At 36 years of age I now work fulltime and have done so since leaving school. Initially in retail, and now as a public servant where I spent the first eight and a half years as an 'Agony Aunt' of sorts as I worked in a call centre for one of the largest local authorities in the country. I spent the majority of the years in that position listening to people moan and complain about their 'first world problems'.

After spending eight and half years working within that section I moved to another more peaceful one within the organisation to which I work. I have spent the past five years in that particular section during which time I have worked hard at obtaining an honours degree in Information Technology Management.

This was a massive achievement for me as I ultimately want to work in the IT field within the organisation I work for.

The time that I had spent in that call centre led me to two conclusions about my life up until that point. Firstly, how strong and resilient I had become over the years prior, and secondly, whenever I felt like giving up or effectively 'throwing in the towel' I would always remember those words that a young boy dressed as an old man told his god like son..."*A man's got to do, what a man's got to do*".

Conclusion

To summarise the original concept behind this book, and its deeply rooted sole purpose, I will end with this. True empowerment is not only isolated to the aforementioned characteristics as highlighted within the previous chapters contained within this book; but fundamentally reliant on one other characteristic as well, with that being *strength*. The strength that I am referring to is not that of the physical world that we inhabit, but that of the mental one that lies inside us all.

We can have all the correct amounts of positive *attitude* in the world, but this is to no avail if we do not have an equally adequate inner strength to match this.

We can show unquestionable levels of physical and or mental *bravery* in the face of an obstacle, but this can be in vain if we are not strong enough to back it up with action.

We can be as clever as we require, through learning, and then subsequently face the world with our newfound *intelligence*. However, this can be ignorant of us to do if we do not have the strength to learn from the mistakes that we have, and will continue to make within all of our lives.

We can *love* others as much as we feel is necessary, but can still fail to have the inner strength required of us to love ourselves, more than we have love for the external world in which we physically inhabit.

We can possess the greatest *imagination* in the world; yet fail to see our dreams become reality due to a lack of strong self-belief in all that we are capable of doing.

While showing *tenacity* may demonstrate a person who bounces back from rejection much easier, strength is about guaranteeing to both yourself; and the world, that you *do not fall so easily*.

To truly know ourselves internally, and embrace and then subsequently express our *identities* without fear of judgement and ridicule requires a massive amount of strength; this should go without saying.

Lastly, as citizens of this world; and regardless of where exactly in the world we are living, we all have rights. However, sometimes we may need to fight to guarantee that these rights are adhered to by those in power. While fighting for the *equality* that we may desperately seek, it will also obviously require an individual who demonstrates pure unwavering strength.

I am not saying that strength is the most important value of all; this is simply not the case, as they are all just as important, while also being reliant and dependable upon one another. What I am saying is that if you have, or can begin to expand on the already existing characteristics as highlighted within this book; and then *show true strength* through the *actions you take*, then that is *true empowerment*, and you will be empowered, regardless of your ability.

EMPOWERING ABILITIES

- Voices of the Voiceless –

Bonus Chapter One – *"CANdemic"*

By Kathryn Hogan, Aine Lawlor & Niamh Dunphy

Introduction

By Tracey Mccann

Hello I trust that you have been enjoying this book so far. How are you feeling? Inspired? Empowered? Love? Joyful? What thoughts come in mind from reading these authors incredible journeys?

So now onto the next part of this book…thee 'bonus' chapters. I hope you feel so far that this 'Empowering Abilities' book has been created good. I trust too that you noticed if you take the first letter from each chapter title that has been written by a particular author ultimately it spells out the word 'ABILITIES', and that the preface was titled 'Empowering'.

After the main body of the book was complete in 2020 I strongly believed that this book had come together quite successfully. However, I noticed that my creative ideas were still seeping through as the final chapter became complete, and I had this inspiring thought for creating another book tailored specifically around the lockdown… and hearing specifically from people with disabilities regarding how they have coped during the whole situation.

As sometimes happens to me when I complete one big project (such as the Empowering Abilities book you have just read) I instantly had an idea for yet another book which was to be the *'Lockdown Empowering Abilities'* book with each of the first letters for the chapter titles spelling out the word *'Lockdown'*. I also thought about releasing it in a few years from now… when everything settles down However it then dawned on me that we have no idea what tomorrow may bring, or our futures will be like. To be honest my hope is for a brighter one, I trust and believe that goodness and more love is coming. It is just a matter of staying connected with yourself and believing in better days ahead… right?

Better days are coming, yes.

I began feeling that I did not want the lockdown book hanging around me while I temporarily prioritized the Empowering Abilities book… leaving the author involved in the Lockdown book waiting in anticipation like, for a while, the authors for Empowering Abilities felt they were. So, Patrick and I decided to put together what we had for the Lockdown book and place it as bonus chapter in this Empowering Abilities book. I honestly feel it worked out perfectly with author numbers, page count, and content.

I trust that everything is ALWAYS working out.

The lockdowns experienced around the globe were a bit of a challenge for everyone, however from hearing from different individuals with disabilities, or individuals who support the disabled we may get the impression that for some, their lives had not really changed; whilst for others the changes were massive. This knowledge should now open you up to the two-tiered world that existed during these lockdowns… and that what we may all take for granted…can be easily taken a way.

For me, I love my independence and I know you do too. During the lockdown I found more things more of a challenge, and I did feel anxious about doing certain things.

Independence is very important to us all…but especially for the disabled. I felt as though my independence skills, which I had been working on for years, were being tested. However, adapting and learning to overcome obstacles was something that I was accustom to.

I felt the world of the disabled, and the vulnerable, grew that bit smaller for all.

Here is a particular story that I would like to share which really highlights the lack of support and understanding for an individuals required needs.

The story begins a week before my wedding in October 2020, it was a Saturday. I asked my sister in-law would she go into town with me for some wedding bits and girly time, to which she said yes. This bit of quality girl time was something for me to look forward to.

This was my first time on a bus since March as I had just avoided using them completely. Prior to Covid public transport was something that I had always used and I found great joy in going off and observing different people, and different surroundings. So indeed I felt excited to be back on public transport… going for a ramble.

I had wrote out my shopping list so I knew what to get and where to go which was great. Coming to the end of my mini shopping spree however my sister in-law began talking about how she is looking forward to a "cuppa coffee". I said "I want to get a cuppa too". I had this perfect image of us going into the cafe and me getting a glass with a handle, and both of us sitting in the cafe with me being able to use my phone on the table to communicate properly. However, I completely forgot the Level 3 restrictions which hampered my plans for sitting in-doors, and also they only had paper cups available in the cafe. I had not bothered bringing my glass with the handle, which I require, because walking around for a few hours with it in my bag would have made my shoulder sore. In the instance of realization as to what this meant for me I did suffer a certain level of anxiety and began thing thinking 'how will I manage?'

We then looked for seats in the shopping centre but they were gone and so we went outside. I said "I'll just have it here". I had gotten a hot chocolate as I am not a coffee drinker and I had two paper cups.

I was really looking forward to it and my sister in-law poured a bit into the one of the paper cups which she then placed into my hand. I had to really try and grip the paper cup from the bottom and get it up to my mouth…this was really difficult, especially on a very busy street with some passersby asking for spare change and others asking if I am ok? Do I have I tooth ache? During this I was just trying to keep in the laughter… and this made me laugh even more. I knew when I removed the cup from my mouth that I would have a chocolate mustache, and chocolate would be roll down my neck. When I did remove the cup from my mouth I looked at my reflection in a nearby shop window and indicated to my sister in-law to get me tissue, which I forgot. I was in the corner of this busy street, looking inwards at a shop window, and feeling myself on the verge of have a 'laugh out loud' moment. I was visualising how this may look from the perspective of others, and then of course to make matters worse it began to rain. My sister in-law came back with a handful of tissue and managed to rescue my face. We then moved into a hallway of a nearby shopping centre and I want to try again and once again she poured a bit of my drink into the cup and I grip it. Now however anytime I attempt at having a sip of my drink I laugh at the challenge of it, made more difficult by supposed curious onlookers. I knew that this was more stress than it was ultimately worth… but again…I try… even if just for a taste, to quench my thirst even a small bit. However, I could not drink it all. I did laugh at the inconvenience of it…that is all you can do really.

I was dressed up very smart for the day and all and that went downhill, of course… I just had to roll with it.

It was far from an ideal 'cuppa hot chocolate', after a lovely shopping experience with my sister in-law. But I really thought at the time, that there should have been more available during the lockdowns. Especially for people who really need access to facilities to socialise or even just have a drink. People who would find it difficult to drink and eat while walking or standing, without anything to lean on, or even a seat and a table in a nice environment would have been great.

I am sure a lot would agree that during the lockdowns the simplest of things became a struggle for most...and near impossible for some.

On the bright side of that story I did manage to have a good laugh from it, even a few days after, because all you can do is laugh… and ***not feel defeated,*** right?

The Positive Aspect of the Lockdowns

For me personally the positive side of the lockdowns were that they enabled me to put my full concentration into starting my own 'official' business which subsequently allowed me to demonstrate, to myself and others, my true capabilities. I even took the massive leap of going that one step further and registering my business, 'Empowering Abilities', with both the CRO (Companies Registration Office) and Revenue.

After this was complete I honestly felt as though I was both taking myself seriously and more passionate, but also was going to be taking much more seriously by my hopeful future clientele. At time I was also more eager towards being creative and figuring out exactly 'how' I can serve people in the best way possible.

During the lockdowns my fitness really developed due to entering into a local community run gym which began running external finesses classes in the great outdoors. This made me very grateful to have this new experience that I was longing for. It enabled me to build up new fantastic connections, with the right supportive and fun people. To then train in locations that I never thought were on my door step was incredible. Due to this gym I also got into running, big time, and I took part in a half marathon from Finglas to Howth… and then a full marathon in Belfast.

Within this gym there is great support, and training in the buildup to every challenge we take on as a group. Being part of this gym has made me feel so alive, healthy and very thankful for the friendships that I created.

Aside from my own personal achievements made during the lockdowns I also witnessed Patrick getting through his honors degree, while working from home. During the latter part of his final year in college he really struggled with the isolation he was enduring having to do all of this from home…on his own.

To witness his determination as he and he alone was the only real person pushing him day-in and day-out was inspiring. Patrick wanted to achieve getting his degree because it was also a personal achievement for him. This was due to the fact that the school he went to did not have the leaving certificate has an option for students. To me that did not seem fair as the way I perceived it is that the intellectual capabilities were defined based on the physical disabilities. In Patricks' case it proves that you can create your own reality, and not one based upon another's perception of your capabilities. Patrick went out and made it his mission to achieve this goal…all while facing the additional stresses he endured during the lockdown.

Just like others who decided to keep going…so did Patrick. It is great to see Patrick smiling with pride over this accomplishment, and I feel so proud to share this with you.

"The Limit Does Not Exist"
By Kathryn Hogan

My name is Kathy Hogan and I am a 29 year old Mom of two. I am also a carer to my six year old son Devin Thomas.

Devin was flagged for ASD (or more commonly known as Autism) at his two year developmental check. The year following was a tough one for us all, we attended appointment after appointment to get Devin on track and most importantly intervene as early as possible.

Devin was diagnosed with Autism Spectrum Disorder on the 30th of April 2018.

Due to all the help we got from the REIS team and (most importantly) all of the effort and work Devin put in himself through endless appointments with many different specialists, now Devin speaks like any other six year old his age. Devin can now also attend mainstream school like most of his peers, but this is not without struggle for him. All of these day-to-day struggles that Devin faces are what he can handle on a "normal" basis; throw a pandemic and the subsequent three lockdowns into the mix and you soon realise how far your limits can go.

In March 2020 we were all aware of the coronavirus, but not what was to unfold in the coming months. By the 12th of March schools and workplaces were beginning to shut down and slowly home began to feel like prison. The lack of routine for Devin, routine that we tirelessly built for, had been completely undone. As any parent with a child with Autism will know, routine is one of the most important aspects of life for an Autistic child.

Caring for Devin in this situation (along with breast feeding my six month old daughter) meant that even the most menial day-to-day tasks became a massive struggle.

It also started to become noticeable that the anxiety within Devin had intensified and night terrors were a common nightly occurrence. By April 2020 I had both children sleeping in my bed, one waking every two hours to be fed, and one waking up in sheer terror, screaming because of the stage his anxiety had gotten to.

After many phone calls to Devin's psychologist and a lot of strategies tried it still felt we were getting nowhere, the pandemic and the lockdowns cast a shadow over the once happy place that we called home.

When schools reopened in September I thought that this would help our home situation but unfortunately for Devin he had become accustomed to being by my side day in and day out.

Every single morning without fail Devin would scream, cry and panic at the school gates, not wanting to leave me or his sister. He was always the last to go in, with the help of the school staff. You would think this would subside as the weeks went on but unfortunately it did not…as this also became another everyday occurrence.

Just as we began to see a slight change in Devin's behavior and we started to get him to fall asleep in his own bed again the schools once again shut their doors due to this virus, which was **not just a virus that affected the respiratory system… but had now also had a detrimental effect on each and everyone's mental health.**

During this third lockdown which we felt was the worst for us, myself and Devin seemed to clash a lot. This was because the person who was supposed to be his Mammy had now also become his full time school teacher, a role I was not prepared for… and neither was he. Devin could not seem to make sense as to why he now had to do his school work at the kitchen table as this was not the environment that he was used to learning in.

After three weeks of constant back and forth arguments and tears on both mine and Devin's behalf… I had to pack in my role as teacher and just focus on being mammy again. Unfortunately this meant that when Devin eventually went back to school he was very behind from his peers… and the catch up game was a whole new struggle in itself.

This struggle was something I knew that he felt. Due to this struggle he felt as though he was not good enough or confident enough to get back to the level he was previously at. Let me tell you something… when you look into your five year old sons eyes and you see the pain and defeat that this lack of confidence has caused in him… this had started me questioning my own ability as a parent.

Fortunately things started to improve in June of this year when I managed to save enough money to finally get my first car and have the means to start Devin in a beautiful country school, with a brilliant ASD unit and also an amazing understanding of children with Autism that attend mainstream classes. Since starting this school in September, Devin has gone from strength-to-strength and can now even write his own name. This is all because of the help he has received since September. On the day that I am writing this very piece my beautiful little boy came running in the front door grinning from ear-to-ear as he eagerly blurted out, and with pride in his eyes, that he had received student of the week.

A very proud moment… for a very tired mammy.

If it is one thing that these lockdowns have taught us it is that even the most normal everyday battles, as hard as they are, can still be fought and we can still come out on top. Just like with Devin… who now sleeps in his own bed, and whose anxieties have slightly subsided.

A boy who is back to laughing, and smiling every day. He demonstrates to us all, in my honest opinion, that **even though the limits were put on our movements, and no matter how tough things got, or how many times we wanted to throw in the towel....that limits do not exist.**

EMPOWERING ABILITIES

- Voices of the Voiceless –

Courage

By Aine Lawlor

My name is Aine Lawlor and I am a special Olympian. I was born with a rare syndrome known as 22q. This syndrome is the consequence of a missing piece of a genetic chromosome essential for development. Most individuals have 23 fully intact pairs of chromosomes, making a total of 46 altogether. However due to this syndrome, I am missing a small piece of my 22th chromosome. As with a large amount of genetic disabilities the side effects of this syndrome can vary… I have only mild side-affects. Thankfully this means that I am still able to have an active life, work and participate in Special Olympics events. Still however, I must endure a daily fight with the side-affects incurred due to my 22q diagnoses. The daily obstacles and challenges to which I am referring to include low muscle tone, arthritis, tummy issues, and ear nose and throat infections. However, to me and those who know me, 22q is just the name of my syndrome… it is not the name for me.

My Mam is the founder of '22q11 Ireland' group which is the only charity group for this syndrome within Ireland. All of the fundraising events are done by the Mams and Dads of those affected by this syndrome. Within this group there also exists a young adult group called 'Yeep Group' which is a collection of young experienced expert panel to which I am the ambassador for. I use my voice to help others with this syndrome.

Aside from my advocate work I also enjoy physical fitness and as previously indicated am involved in Olympic level sport. My particular sport of interest is ten pin bowling. I also work part-time in a creche.

The pandemic was very hard at the beginning as we just did not know what would happen next…and unfortunately we are still living like this to an extent. It was, and still is, tough and difficult. The whole nation shut down as we were heading unwillingly into the unknown. For me personally, at the beginning I did not know how to handle my stress, anxiety and depression. But thank goodness for fitness as my local gym in Ballybough saved me. They evolved to the requirements and restrictions very quickly and managed to run work-outs via zoom, which was good for me as it enabled me to still get to see all my friends, even if just virtually as opposed to in-person. Human-to-human interaction matters, regardless of the method. This form of interaction enabled me to control my anxiety. Physical fitness did this too, via walking and Yoga etc. Never in my life had I done Yoga before and now I love it. Also, to control any bad thoughts that may have crept into my mind, I took up colouring mindfulness things to help calm me down. That really helped. I then began thinking more positively and began to feel a lot better.

I had family and friends to have zoom chats with and that helped me greatly as I got my emotions 'off my chest'. I always find it important to tell your family or friends how you are feeling.

I would tell them how and why I was finding things a lot different and a lot harder as I could not see my friends, or family, or be with my Special Olympics friends as my training sessions had stopped during the lockdowns. That hurt the most…and it still does to be honest.

On a positive note however, I have now learnt how to 'adapt to change', as I was previously never good at accepting such large scale changes within my life. I learned a life lesson in this simple fact… sometimes **change is good, you just have to open your eyes to see it…and open your heart to accept it.**

Kids with 22q

A Poem by Aine Lawlor

"Kids with 22q need to believe in themselves and they need to believe in their dreams, their goals. They need to believe that they can have a life like everyone else, get married, have kids and have a job. They need to believe in themselves. They need to believe that they can do well in school – they can go to college and get an education.

Parents need to believe in kids, need to respect their kids. They needs to accept the fact that their child has22q or their child won't be able to live their life.
When the parent accepts it the child will too. Most number one thing to do – accept what you have. You do that and your life will change."

Written in 2010 by Aine Lawlor.
#22qAwarenessDays

Bowling Ireland Games Limerick 2014
By Aine Lawlor

You got to take a deep breath,

because this is your chance grab it with all your might,

stay calm and fight.

This is where your strong not weak.

It's a dream you seek one shot

Make it good,

Make the crowd see what bowling is meant o be

Win or lose it doesn't matter

This sport is like climbing a ladder.

Just make sure to have fun and a blast,

Just know YOU are a champion at heart.

Hold it there and when it's your time to shine,

Shine bright, that's when your gonna wake.

That's when it's YOUR moment to take.

EMPOWERING ABILITIES

- Voices of the Voiceless –

Keep Going
By Niamh Dunphy

My name is Niamh Dunphy and I'm a 24-year-old podcaster, blogger and university student. I have recently completed a Bachelor of Arts Honours degree in digital marketing in TU Dublin Tallaght campus. At the beginning of the coronavirus pandemic in March 2020 I felt a mixture of emotions because I wasn't aware how serious the coronavirus was much like many people in the country at the time and was unsure how it would impact my life. However, I also welcomed it as slight opportunity to recover from a foot operation that I had had the month before the pandemic began. Like everyone I did feel anxiety but not for the reasons you might think. I live independently with the assistance of carers and I was worried about how this completely unknown situation would impact the biggest aspect of my life. As this situation was completely new to the whole country and nobody knew how to prepare for it, I didn't know how that would impact me. Thankfully, everything has run about as normally as it could have for the care side of things during these times, however, I always have a backup plan in case something goes wrong.

The biggest change was adapting to online learning. While this was a struggle for every student in the country, for students with disabilities this change was massive. For example, in a regular college day my academic PA is not only my note taker but they also tend my personal needs such as toileting throughout the day when I'm on campus.

Due to the government restrictions, I had a note taker who sat in on my classes via Microsoft Teams and assisted me with assignments through this method also. While this meant I was able to keep on equal academic par with my classmates, unfortunately, this change meant that the ability for my academic PA to tend to my personal care needs during the day was gone. This was probably the biggest change that I had to adapt to as it meant I had to tailor my homecare package to suit my needs as best as possible. I developed a lot of mental strength from this situation and everything that came with it to be able to be a bit more open when it comes to speaking about my needs and how to improve them and also knowing that it was okay to speak in the times that I wasn't feeling in the best headspace because of this situation to get the help that I needed. In terms of actual academic support, I found it easier to learn and work remotely as due to a change in the restrictions from September onwards I was allowed to have my academic PA at home with me. I found this easier than a normal learning environment because I could speak to my PA while she was taking notes if I didn't understand something or wanted any extra notes added in whereas normally in a lecture hall I would have to whisper to my PA while the lecturer speaks. During this time, I also learned to be appreciative of the amount of work that goes on behind the scenes to help me complete my degree. For example, through the lockdown I was given an academic support hour every week. This was to help me ensure that I was fully understanding the assignments that were being given to me and completing them to my full potential as well as giving me a space to vent to my support lecturer if I was finding things tough.

I feel very fortunate to have accommodations like this be given to me without hesitation as students with disabilities may sometimes need just a little bit more understanding of our situations than we're willing to ask for.

In terms of general life as a person with a disability I think the majority of things stayed the same for me anyway. Due to the fact that I live with the assistance of carers most of my life has to be planned from what time I get up in the morning to what time I got to bed at night. However, I am stubbornly independent and this means that I am used to the things that I noticed people getting irritated by during the pandemic such as only being able to stay at a restaurant for a certain period of time. As this is normal for me due to the fact that I have to ensure that I'm home in time for my last care call at night. However, the most difficult thing for me was not seeing my friends, family or boyfriend. Particularly my sister and nieces who live in London as they're only young, being far away kind of makes you feel like you're missing out on the most exciting years of their life as they develop their own personalities as well as that. It was the simple stuff that I missed like being able to go for a Nando's with my friends and catch up on the craziness that goes on in their lives when we don't see each other or my uncle popping in for his weekly chat and an ice cream.

I decided to take this very unpredictable time as an opportunity to try out some new creative ideas that I normally wouldn't have the time to do such as launching a podcast. Before Covid I was very heavily involved in my universities radio society. I did a radio show called Irish Music Gems where I interviewed up and coming Irish talent about their music. It was the one thing I was really starting to miss during lockdown so I decided to turn it into a podcast. This gave me the opportunity to keep doing something that I've always enjoyed and has kept me positive in difficult times before the pandemic as I find it to be a good way of expressing myself. The flexibility of it being my own podcast meant that I could record interviews around my care and at times that suited both me and the guests. This allowed me to feel pride and in control of a creation that was mine as it is an outlet where I don't feel aware of the physical restrictions of my disability. Starting the podcast has also given me the opportunity to network and form friendships with people of similar interests to me. In the beginning this was just a very random idea that I wanted to use to bring some positivity into people's lives during the uncertain times of lockdown, however, nearly a year later I've made some great friends, been asked to guest on other people's podcasts and have opened a lot of doors for myself within creative industries. I feel very grateful and very privileged that one simple idea has brought me so much positivity and happiness.

For me each of the lockdowns were individually tough in their own way at times for a lot of the reasons I have already mentioned, but the people that have been a very big support in the times that I don't publicly show on social media or speak about were my auntie Kathleen, Uncle Tom and friend Helena. Someone told me once that in times of crisis the people that have known you for your whole life are the ones that you turn to. I've been very lucky to have particularly these three people in my life who have known me for my whole life to support me through the battle that life can be at times, let me vent when I'm angry and remind me that they're proud of me after every achievement. I think that as we get older and grow as people and learn more about ourselves, we achieve everything with the support of the people that have been there through the good, bad and uncertain times and I'm grateful that these people in particular and many more that I don't have room to mention have been around through all of those times. In terms of keeping myself motivated not only during the pandemic, but all the way through my life I have lived with the attitude of never being afraid to try anything. This is simply because everything that I've ever tried not thinking much of doing it at the time has given me some incredible experiences. Although, that could also be down to my unique way of looking at the world and feeling the need to try every completely crazy idea that's ever come into my head just to see how it would work out and every time it either gives me a funny memory that I hold with me forever or an unforgettable experience.

I chose "Keep Going" as my chapter to write for this book mostly because I think even pre-Covid it's something that I've always done throughout my whole life even when times were difficult. I think I've always been determined to do everything that I can regardless of how tough things were. I personally found the pandemic productive but maybe I wouldn't have if I didn't do as the title of this chapter says and *just keep going*.

The following chapter is an exact replication of a piece of work written in 2003 by Jennifer (Jenny) McCann. Jenny experienced many struggles in her life of which you will soon discover, however Jenny met those struggles and challenges with a positive, tenacious, strong, and self-empowered mental attitude. She loved and was equally loved by all those who had the privilege to cross her path. Jenny's seemingly never ending smile and positivity lit up the darkest of rooms upon her entry. The following piece of work was written over 17 years ago by a young woman who experienced more trauma than most. In my honest opinion it summarises life itself which I am certain that we can all agree is not easy...but life is never always too difficult either. Life contains many moments of both sunshine, and rain...

"Life is a storm, my young friend. You will bask in the sunlight one moment, be shattered on the rocks the next. What truly defines you is what you do when that storm comes. You must look into that storm and shout....Do your worst, for I will do mine! Then the fates will know you as we know you"

- Alexander Dumas (The Count of Monte Cristo)

EMPOWERING ABILITIES

- Voices of the Voiceless –

Bonus Chapter Two – "Sunshine and Rain"
By Jennifer (Jenny) McCann

"I am not Dystonia…I am much, much more!"
– Jenny McCann

When I Was Small

I was meant to be born on the 10th of April and my cousin Richard was meant to be born on 20th but we swapped dates! I made a grand entrance but I was ten days late. I had jet black hair and weighed 8 pounds 6 and a half ozs. My Mam and Dad decided to call me Jennifer. Mam warned my aunts, uncles and my grandparents never to shorten my name but who was the one who shortened my name? My Mam of course!

I remember being in a playgroup and my hair was short blonde. I enjoyed painting. I remember going to see Bosco with all my friends and sitting on the floor and Bosco saying 'Look behind you'.

My Mam and Dad always brought Stephen and I on trips to all the parks and the zoo. I liked the parks because I could climb the trees.

I had a lot of dolls and a pram. I didn't play with them much. I played on my bike and liked water-play and paining the best.

I was sometimes naughty, as I wouldn't do as I was told and stuck out my tongue. I put salt instead of sugar in my Mam and Dad's tea. Once I put an ice pop in their bed and it melted and it was sticky when they got in! The next thing I remember is going to school. It was great because when I saw the toys around like in playgroup. I wasn't worried and I didn't even say good-bye to my Mam!

Two weeks after I started school, I woke up during the night and knew something was wrong. I don't know how but I knew that my Dad had died. Grandma came to help look after us for a few weeks. I miss my Dad very much. Dad always brought me for walks and we played ball and skipped stones in the Dodder river.

A lot of our relations visited us at first but then they stopped coming. We always went to visit them. We always got lots of food and sweets but sometimes it was boring sitting around.

I can still remember some things from when I was small. I love it when Mam tells me about them and also looking at photos. I have both happy and sad memories but it's good to have them.

Growing Up

When I was young, even though I was extremely shy, I still got involved in the community. I joined Irish dancing with my friends. A few weeks into it my friends left, leaving me on my own. Even though they had left, I kept it up.

I entered competitions. I won a few trophies and medals, and I even went on the St Patrick's Day parade. I thought I was the bees' knees waving and dancing in the street.

I left a few weeks after the parade, and I joined Brigins. We had to wear a horrible brown uniform, beige knee high socks and black shoes. I had a sleeve almost full of badges that I had to work hard for. I went away on camps with my two friends Michelle and Ciara. The place we stayed in was a very old house that had three floors, very creepy and cold. In the night our group would get up to mischief. We got make up and went into the other girls' room. While the girls were sleeping, we drew on their faces. It was brilliant.

After that I started the Girls Guides because I was too old for Brigins. I really enjoyed the Girl Guides too. As a group we entered competitions. Even though we lost most of them we still had a laugh, particularly when we played a game similar to musical chairs. The floor was very slippery and our team was slipping and sliding everywhere.

My all time favourite hobby was art. If I were bored I would spend most of my time in my room, lying down on the floor drawing. I read books like the "Famous Five" and books about animals which I really enjoyed. I also played Mammies and Daddies mainly on my own! I would make a 'pretend car' with two chairs. Outside I enjoyed cycling around on my bike. I loved having races with my friends. Everyone on the road would play rounders. I thought I was a deadly pitcher.

I always loved animals. We had two cats called Ebony and Puss 'n Boots and a dog-called Pepe. We also had some wild cats out our back. I liked spending time with them. Pepe was a strong dog. I always took him for a walk down to the local park, beside the river Dodder. While he was running around I would be talking to myself.

I loved Pepe but one day he had to go to a new home because he was attacking people. I was very upset. My friend Carrie (6) kept me company and gave me a hug. Carrie said 'Pepe will be fine'. To-day I still miss him.

I really enjoyed school. I was an early riser. I would get up at 5 but wouldn't have to be in school until 9 o'clock! I just had to be on time! My friends would always be 5 minutes late. I was panicking in case I would get into trouble because I was late.

How Life has Changed for Me

It was the weekend — the last weekend in September. I got a terrible pain in my little finger on my left hand. Mam took me up to my local GP. When I saw him, he said it's only a sprain and strapped my fingers together.

It was Monday morning, I got up at 5 o'clock ready for school and I was starting second year in secondary school. When Mam got up and saw me she said, "You stay at home!" as I didn't seem well. I said 'OK' and lay on the bed. When the pain got worse, Mam got worried.

She rang Mary to tell her I was ill and she wouldn't be able to come into work. Mary said "Don't worry about getting a taxi, I have the car and it will be quicker for me to drop you both into the hospital". It seemed like I was waiting forever; when I tried to stand my feet just went from under me. Mam came in and I heard her saying " you have every symptom of meningitis except for the rash". My Grandma, who has sadly since, died, and Granddad had come up for a visit. They got a shock when they saw me. They said to Mam "You get Jenny into hospital and we will look after Stephen", Stephen is my brother. Mam had to shadow walk me out to the car. The last words I said were "It really hurts Ma"

I have not spoken clearly since that day.

Dystonia October 1ˢᵗ 1997.

I got every test done but they came back clear. It was good in one way but not in another way because we still didn't know what was wrong. Some weeks passed on. A doctor called Dr Webb came in and said "I have seen something similar in Great Ormond Street Hospital". It's 'called Dystonia'. Mam and I looked at each other as if to say WHAT! Dr Webb explained what it was. He found out what type I had, he said 'Rapid Onset Dystonia Parkinisom'. A year later my brother Stephen was diagnosed with Dystonia.

I was very upset because I didn't want to see him go through what I had. To lose his speech would have been harder for him than for me because he had learning difficulties too. Stephen was lucky because the type he got is called "Hemidystonia", which only affects his left side and doesn't affect his speech. I gave a sigh of relief.

We found out through a family meeting, that other members from my Dad's side of the family were affected too, including my Dad. I knew you couldn't die from it. When Dad was alive, he went through everything I did. The Doctor's just said "it's all in your head, Fran" and gave him different types of medicine including Steroids. The Doctors only told my Mam that Dad had Dystonia when I was diagnosed. Apparently he died from complications from Dystonia and the wrong drugs. They just told Mam and Dad (back when he was ill) he was making it up and go home. Dad got worse over the next two and a half years and finally collapsed. I was very angry when I found out. I still am because if they just listened to him and knee what was wrong, he might still be alive today.

Wheelchair User

I was always curious about people in wheelchairs, never thinking it would happen to me. I had this chair it was like an armchair on wheels. Mam use to push me up and down the corridors in the chair. I was in that much pain, I didn't mind being in it.

Then a few months down the line, Dr Webb decided, I was allowed out for a walk for a few hours a day. I was delighted with that. I used a normal wheelchair for going out, I wore a big heavy coat, a hat, a blanket rapped around my legs and I also had a horrible feeding tube sticking out from my nose. I looked like an old granny. I found people staring at me. I was saying in my head "stop looking at me". I used to get very angry, frustrated and upset and said "why me"? I still hate the way people stare at me when I'm a wheelchair user. They treat me like a baby and talk to whoever is pushing me instead of talking to me. They sometimes pat me on the head as if I'm a dog. If someone asks how I am my Mam says "Ask Jenny yourself!" Sometimes doors are too small for a wheelchair to fit through or shops are too crowded and I have to stay outside the shop. I would love to look around the shop and not be restricted.

Lost speech

The hardest thing for me to take was when I lost my speech. My body was so stiff; I couldn't even shake my head to say 'yes' or no. It was very frustrating. The speech therapist put a chart of sign language on my door to communicate with the nurses, doctors and my visitors. One dreadful time I had a one –to- one nurse to give Mam a break. In the morning she was brushing my teeth. The dozy nurse brushed them with Clearasil (a skin cream). I was doing my sign for 'NO, STOP' but she insisted: 'You have to get your teeth cleaned'. When my family came up to visit me. I told them what happened. They were Furious!

Pain

At the beginning the pain was extreme. Did you ever get a cramp? Well it's like that, but I had it all over my body. I still do, but not as severely now. The doctor couldn't give me anything for it because they didn't know what was wrong. Mam would be coming in the front door of the hospital and she could hear me screaming with the pain. St Michael's ward, where I was, was at the back of the hospital.

The loss of friends

I was in secondary school; I had a few friends from my year. When I got Dystonia they all disappeared off the face of the earth. One teacher, Trish, stuck with me through thick and thin. When I finally got out of hospital, Trish would take me out in her car. Trish still comes and takes me out. One day she brought up three girls from my school up to visit me. Cathrina, Emily and Karen were a year ahead of me, I knew them to see but I soon got to know them. They still keep in touch and take me out. One time Trish asked me "where would you like to go today" I said "I would love to go visit the school and my year". When I got there it felt strange! They were all waiting, they gave me gifts. After that visit we went back for a few more visits. I was invited to go to the debs. I was chuffed. I brought Richard (my boyfriend) with me. Some of the students were talking to me as if I were brain dead, I just laughed it off. It was great to see everyone, very enjoyable and emotional – but I found that I did get very upset.

National Rehabilitation Hospital

There were only seven children in the Children's ward, which wasn't too crowded. Most of the patients in the hospital had been in car accidents. The Staff were wonderful and great company.

The seven of us had a timetable for different things we had to do during the day. **I had to learn everything again.** In the mornings we had our breakfast and got everything we needed for the day. Next I went to physio. My physio was Vanda. She had me walking everywhere on my walker. I felt very independent. School next, where I worked mainly on the computer: speech were Siobhan thought me how to say 'c' words. Then we had dinner and went for relaxation time. I sometimes nodded off.

In the afternoons we went back to school. Every afternoon we had a different activity like drama or sports. When school was finished I went to O. T. Susan was my O. T, she taught me how to use my feet like on the computer, painting and draughts because I couldn't use my hands very well. I also did cooking and tile-making where I made teapot stands.

When everything was finished up we all went upstairs, did our homework and had our tea and we could do whatever we wanted. I played games with Mary and Niamh (two patients in the ward).

Then I went looking for favourite male nurse (Peter), who worked on the men's ward, which was beside the children's ward. Peter knew I fancied him and he took me out to the pictures one night; I really enjoyed it.

I went home at weekends. I spent a year out there. In that time Mam would come out nearly every day to visit me. She also rang when she couldn't make it.

On my last day there, they gave a big party because I was one of longest patients in there. They all gave me gifts including Peter. I was sad to be leaving and happy to be going home. I burst into tears when my taxi came and wouldn't let Peter go. To this day I still miss everyone.

The National Rehabilitation Hospital is the best!!

New School, New Friends

It was Monday morning in February. I was starting a new school, Scoil Mochua for the physically disabled. I got upset because I didn't want to go to a disabled school; I wanted to go back to Firhouse Community College. Mam comforted me and said "I know it's hard love but you will make new friends". After a while I calmed down. I had to go to the school in a taxi because I wasn't on the transport list as yet.

I was a little bit nervous at first. My teacher was Anthony and my classmates were James, Paul, Gerard, Brian, Michelle and Aine. The classroom assistant was Grainne. They made me feel very welcome by introducing their friends to me and having a good laugh with them. I soon got to know them. When I got home I had a big smile on my face and the first thing I said was "That school is deadly" to my Mam.

Time passed, students left and I got to know more students, teachers and assistants, who are helpful, caring and a great laugh. Every morning I would look forward to John White taking me off my bus because he would have me blue in the face from laughter. Because Scoil Mochua is small everyone is close. Nearly everyone is my friend and they understand me. I love Scoil Mochua.

I went on a speech camp. There was only me and this lad called Richard from Scoil Mochua. I only knew Richard to see. The rest of the people were from all over Ireland and the speech therapists were from the C.R.C (another school for physically disabled students). I soon got to know Richard. We had a good laugh and good fun. We became friends. Little did I know that three years later, he was to become my boyfriend. We are now going out with one another over a year.

I went on a few more camps, going out at night and going on school trips. But it's not all about going out it's work too. I enjoy doing schoolwork but my all time favourite subjects are English and Art. When my friends were doing the Junior Cert, I couldn't do it because I hadn't got the energy. But just there last year I did two subjects from the Junior Cert; English, C.S.P.E and a project on Art, which was a Fetac project. In September, I got the results, I got an A in both Junior Cert subjects and passed the Art project. I was over the moon with the results. We are doing the Junior Cert music this year. I'm enjoying it.

Last year I went swimming with my class and my Mam came to help. All I was doing was water aerobics, which was good for Dystonia. I never thought I would be able to swim again. This year only six of us go swimming at a time and we take turns. Our swimming instructor Johnny tries to get us as independent as possible. Now I don't use the hoist, I go in off the side. I can walk across the pool, hold onto the bar with one hand, float and then go into standing position. I do have a helper that just puts one hand on my back while I'm kicking my way across and when I'm getting out I walk up the steps with a bit of help. Now I know I can do it, I'm more determined every week.

I love swimming.

I'm on the wheelchair hurling team. Ena (My teacher) pushes me around in my wheelchair and Ena and I can work great together. Ena calls me **"The Lethal Foot"** because I use my right foot even though it's hurling we're playing! I get stuck in and I have never been bruised. We all work great as a team. I also play the odd football game, I play in defence. I have a great time and a good laugh with everyone.

Positive Piece

When I was in the National Rehabilitation hospital, I learnt how to be more independent and communicate better. In June 1998 I met Sarah Ferguson (Duchess of York) in the hospital. She gave me a signed copy of a book she had written. It was called "The Royal Switch".

Later on that year my Mam got me tickets to see Boyzone! I got a surprise when a limo collected me and we were brought out for a meal with Ronan Keating's family. When we got to the concert we were brought backstage to meet the entire band. My legs were shaking so much (especially when I met Keith Duffy) that I had to be held down. They gave us money to get souvenirs and the concert was brilliant.

In the year 2000 Bertie Ahern presented me with a Bravery Award. We were put up in a hotel for a weekend and brought out for meals, outings and a concert. I met stars of TV, and radio including Samantha Mumba. I was on the Late Late show and talked with Pat Kenny.

It was great to meet and get friendly with the other Bravery Award winners especially Aishling who was in the National Rehabilitation hospital when I was there. I also met the President of Ireland Mary McAleese in Aras an Uachtarain and presented her with a picture.

All of these events were brilliant but the best of all was when the ***"Make a Wish"*** Foundation paid for my Mam and I to go to Florida so I could swim with the dolphins. We visited Animal Kingdom, Sea World and Universal Studios. We had a wonderful time. Everything was so overwhelming especially Discovery Cove where I met Capricorn the Dolphin. He was so gentle when I swam with him. I didn't want to leave him. It was a fantastic experience.

I know that there are things I physically cannot do at the moment. So I try to concentrate on what I can do and enjoy myself. As well as Art, Reading and Writing, I really enjoy sports. I participate in anything I can including hurling, football, and swimming.

I am a member of Dystonia Ireland and I take part in the mini-marathon every year to raise funds for research into Dystonia. My brother Stephen and I also help out by letting people know what Dystonia is and how it can affect you. Brian Kerr is Patron of Dystonia Ireland and attends functions with our group. Which helps a lot.

I am a Leader in the local Foroige youth club and I go to a disco once a month in the I. W. A centre. I have a boyfriend Richard and a lot of friends so I am lucky in that way. I have been picked to go to New York for the ***Irish American Physically Challenged Games.*** It's all happen sometime in 2004 and I'm really looking forward to it.

I am learning how to balance more and use my walker so I don't have to rely on my wheelchair all the time. Recently I managed to clasp my hands together, which is something I couldn't do before.

I am leaving school soon and I will miss everyone but I am also looking forward to new experiences and the challenges to come.

My Ambitions for the Future

First of all regarding my health I would like to be able to walk a lot more than I can at present. Also I would like to be able to talk more clearly.

I have always wanted to work with children. Unfortunately because of my physical limitations that's not possible at the moment.

I love Art and Drama I would like to go to college and learn more about them.

I'm partial to writing and have enjoyed working on my life story. I feel writing improves my self-esteem.

I *really* enjoy watching most sports and hope to be able to continue participating in lots of physical challenges. I am on the Scoil Mochua hurling and football teams and have been known to cause a lot pf "damage" with my lethal right foot. Recently I have become more independent in the swimming pool. There was a time when I thought I never would be able to swim again but now I'm determined to continue improving until I get to Olympic standard.

I'm keen to promote awareness of Dystonia and enjoy fundraising. Every year I do the Women's Mini-Marathon and usually raise over 100 euros. I would like to visit people who are sick or lonely.

I may not be able to do everything all at once, but bit by bit I hope to be able to fulfil my ambitions.

I AM NOT DYSTONIA! I AM MUCH, MUCH MORE!

P.S. Just before my book goes to print I am pleased to announce my engagement to Mr. Richard Redmond on St. Valentine's Day 2004.

Dad

We were a happy little family of four
When we went to the zoo it was like a tour
We had some very joyful times
Especially when my dad sang rhymes

****

Then my dad's health got bad
He could hardly talk, it was so sad
Sometimes he couldn't walk far
And we had to travel by car

****

Then death paid a visit to our home
And our tears like a river did roam
The laughter in our house went missing for a while
But we will never forget our dad's smile

****

We are now a family of three
Because Life's like that you see
We still have lots of joyful times
And always remember dad's rhymes

By Jenny

Note to Reader:

On December 27th 2012 Jenny McCann suddenly and sadly passed away. You may find it surprising that this sad fact was left at the end of a book solely aimed at highlighting empowerment in the face of adversity...but that is the point. Life is short for us all sadly. However it should not be about the amount of years that we have spent on this earth...but instead what we chose to do with the time that we had....so choose wisely...and always choose with the utmost respect for your own values.

Jenny chose to be happy, to be hopeful, and to be excited for her future no matter how uncertain it was. She had spent the briefest of moments in both the sunshine and the rain...and because of that Jenny understood the true value and meaning of the rare humanistic traits of perseverance and gratitude.

Jenny also held true to words that she repeated to herself and to others daily....words that relate to us all in some way, shape or form...words which I will now paraphrase...

We are not our disabilities...for we...

are much, much more...